TAROT ETC.
I AM WITCH

A Memoir By Kyla Edwards

BY KYLA A. N. EDWARDS

One Printers Way
Altona, MB R0G 0B0
Canada

www.friesenpress.com

Copyright © 2024 by Kyla A. N. Edwards
First Edition — 2024

All rights reserved.

No part of this publication may be reproduced in any form, or by any means, electronic or mechanical, including photocopying, recording, or any information browsing, storage, or retrieval system, without permission in writing from FriesenPress.

Based on a true story.
Some names, timelines and circumstances have been changed to protect privacy.

ISBN
978-1-03-831126-9 (Hardcover)
978-1-03-831125-2 (Paperback)
978-1-03-831127-6 (eBook)

1. BODY, MIND & SPIRIT, DIVINATION, TAROT

Distributed to the trade by The Ingram Book Company

This is for you Jack.

M*Y FIRST MEMORIES ARE AT ABOUT* the age of two sitting on the floor looking up at all the people in the dark-hooded robes. Then seeing candle flames flickering with the smells of incense, a big picture of a pentagram with the goat and chanting in the basement of my house.

The Occult has been with me and my way of life since birth, an obvious path of purpose. I remember sneaking my parents' spell books and playing "sacrifice" with my sister when we were about four and six years old, taking turns laying out on the altar and pretending to stab each other. I'm not sure if the game "sacrifice" came from their spell books or if it was something I witnessed or remembered from birth. I remember us trying to pronounce words in the books and reenacting other pictures we saw. I remember drawing pentagrams and sigils from the books in crayon in my coloring books. My mother helped me create my own sigil and seal of power at the age of five which I still use to this day.

I remember casting official spells when I was six. All my barbies in a circle with the star in the middle and me and my Doggy, as my right hand. Doggy is my stuffed dog that I still have today, any magic or innocence of childhood I had remains within her.

I would sneak my parents spell books from the basement and reenact what I witnessed them, and their "friends" often did. I remember drawing out the sigils from the Necronomicon and saying the words which I still know today like a second language "zee keeya kampa…"

I remember the secret meetings, the coven meetings, and all the cars in the driveway when "Uncle Jay" would visit. They spent most of their time in the basement and I would sneak to listen to them and sit halfway down the stairs to hear all the strange words and things they would talk about. I knew my dad and Jay were writing a book. Jay would wear black eye liner and sometimes my dad did too. My Dad had a thick phone book in his desk that held hundreds of names of other Satanists, most of them were in California, and my dad would visit there as often as Jay would visit here. I remember taking trips to Vancouver Island with them as well. I would stay at a motel with a babysitter while they were somewhere else practicing rituals or I would be at other houses with the same people in robes, same candles, same chanting, same smells, and the same goat with the star on the wall.

When I first started to talk as a small child, I started to talk to my dead brother, my secret dead twin brother's ghost, who I now call Jack. I remember him whispering to me and I remember us giggling together. I remember him sitting on my bed with me as I would fall asleep.

When my mother realized what and who I was talking to, it freaked out my mother so bad she smacked my little mouth in shock, and I remember her and my dad just staring at me and my dad saying, "this could be a problem". This was obviously concerning to them considering how my brother possibly met with his demise. Were they afraid that I would remember what happened to him and then the consequences of me remembering?

I remember the smack like it was yesterday. My childhood memory is amazing probably because everything was so traumatic.

After that, whenever I would talk out loud to Jack, my mother would just walk away into another room, or put me in a room and shut the door. So, at a very young age I learned to start keeping Jack to myself.

I showed signs of other psychic abilities and mediumship, (talking to other spirits besides their secret dead son), along with severe sleeping disorders such as sleep walking and insomnia (I had to wear bells on my wrists until I was a teenager), and experienced paranormal things at that young age as well which my parents encouraged and supported, but not when it came to Jack. I feel they obviously knew Jack was my brother, something, someone they had major pain and regret associated with and probably wished to just forget about it.

DADDY

"UNCLE JAY" BEING FIRST, MY DAD was second on the council of 9. Dad held a degree of the second order which is degree of Satanic Warlock & High Priest of the Black Order, Satanic Theology, and the Black Arts. He was dually licensed to sustain ritual performances in the realms in accordance with The Satanic Church.

My handsome devil of a Father Gerald, 1938 – 2002.

Again, I am not a Satanist however I was raised as one, as my parents were both Satanists. Jay and my dad were besties, for a while. I believe my dad left the church when I was about 6 or 7 because I don't have any memories of Jay after that age. I am not a Satanist or identify under any other organized religion as I have never found a label or manmade religion to suit me.

My Dad

My dad was always so proud that we were Welsh. He taught me how to use my Dragon energy from a very young age. "Never let them see you coming, get them before they get you, go for the throat, and remember, hesitation will kill you".

I remember him holding me in his arms when I was about three years old, my parents were having one of their hooded robe coven parties and everyone was running outside in excitement. I remember my dad laughing and asking me" can you see them? Can you see them?!" and yes, I could see them. The whole yard was full of orbs. Big white moving orbs. I remember reaching out to try to touch one and it playfully moved out of reach. I don't know what was going on, but I remember that. He always made sure that he played out scarier events and things as totally normal like Dragon energy and mystery orbs, no big deal. He would take us to see horror movies and laugh and laugh so my sister and I would laugh and laugh too.

My dad never talked about the Church of Satan or his own father, my grandfather. My Dad always spared us the drama and would lovingly gaslight us into other topics of conversation if we had questions about his childhood. I never knew any of my grandparents as they were all dead by the time I came along on both sides of my family. And all my estranged cousins are in England.

My aunt Hildy told me much later in life that my grandfather was insane, he was tortured by "the Dragon" that followed my family from Wales to Canada. My Grandfather often talked out loud to it and would often state that it wouldn't leave him alone. He said it told him to do terrible things, including abusing my grandmother and my aunts. Now knowing about Dragon energy myself, I believe my grandfather was mentally ill and just could not handle the incredible chaos magic that comes with Dragons. I do not blame the Dragon for the trauma that happened to my family. The Dragon has served me well. My dad was 5 out of 6, the second youngest out of six. There was my uncle Myrl the oldest, my aunt Vik, the second oldest, who ran away with the circus when she was 17 for life, two more, Aunts Hildy & Shirly, my dad Gerry, and the youngest aunt Cindy.

One terrible day on our Ravencliff family farm, January 18, 1952, my grandfather listened to the Dragon. My 16yr old aunt Shirly had had enough of the abuse and was packing to run away. My Grandfather walked into her room and shot her with his riffle. My 15-year-old aunt Hildy said she heard her father calling for my 14-year-old dad after the gunshot, "Gerry! Gerry!" and then she heard her father yelling "what have I done? No! No! No!" When my dad got to the bedroom up the stairs, my aunt Hildy heard the shotgun go off again. She thought her father had killed her little brother too until she saw my dad come out of the room sprayed in blood. The police arrested my 14-year-old father for the murder of his father due to an account told by my grandfather's friend about catching my dad taking a shot at his father when the three of them were on a hunting trip a few years before.

My dad testified that when he ran into Shirly's room, his dad pointed the gun at his own head and pulled the trigger taking his head clean off right in front of him. Of course, my dad was let go and charges were dropped. Both my Aunt Shirly and grandfather had their funerals on the same day. However, my grandfather's body was buried outside the cemetery in an unmarked grave due to him committing murder and suicide.

In my minds psychic eye, my dad ran into his sister's room and saw his father bent over in instant regret at what he had done to his daughter, and my dad picked up the gun and finished what he meant to do on that hunting trip those few years ago.

When I went to Ravencliff to feel out the Edwards family massacre on the land and conduct my own paranormal investigation of my own family, it felt like I was welcome there. The house was long gone and nothing but forest where it once stood. Then, I went to the cemetery and found my grandfather's unmarked grave with his headless body inside and I performed a forgiveness ceremony right there. That family trauma ends now, with me. Forever our bloodline will master The Dragon energy, not succumb to it.

My grandmother Dee captured the Dragon that tortured her husband resulting in the death of her daughter in the photograph I found in a family album years later. I couldn't believe what I saw in the picture, the dragon so clearly whispering to my grandfather. My grandmother died so young after this incident no doubt from a broken heart.

My dad is my favorite person on the planet. He made our childhood so amazing, spoiled us rotten and was never ever mean or abusive to us. He was always so much fun, told us amazing stories about the magical animals around Ravencliff. He never spoke to us about the Satanic Church or "uncle" Jay or about his mentally ill father. He would tell us fun stories about his dead sister Shirly, and when I asked how she had died so young, my dad just said, "there was something wrong with her stomach." My grandfather had shot her in the stomach. The picture I added of Aunt Shirly, has a clear streak of white to exactly where she was shot in the stomach not long after the picture was taken. And although my dad could have said terrible things about my mother, he never did.

my grandfather and the gun he used to shoot and kill my aunt Shirley and then himself.

my aunt Shirly.
This photo was taken one month before her murder possibly a warning as the streak of mysterious light is the exact trajectory of where she was shot.

Tarot Etc. I Am Witch.

My Grandfather's Dragon

My Dragons show up once and a while in photographs.

Edwards family grave and the beautiful pink orb of gratitude for the forgiveness ceremony

Grandfather's unmarked grave where I performed the forgiveness ceremony

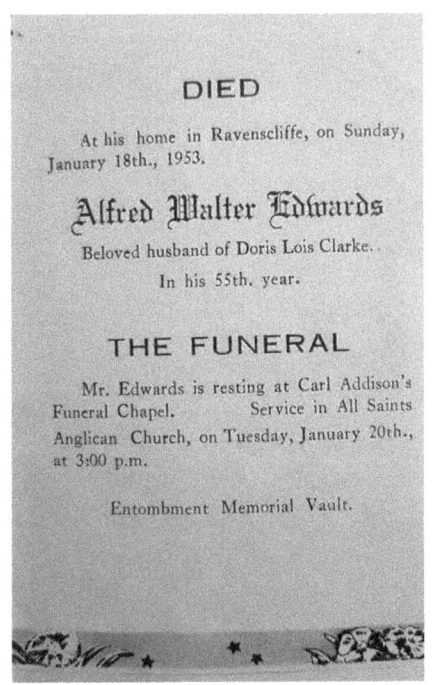

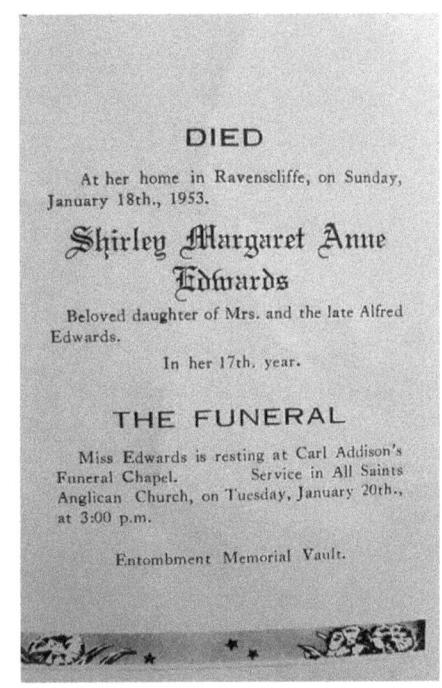

LINORA

My Mother

A Satanic Witch

1942 – 2010 October Blood Moon

MY MOTHER PUT A FULL ON stop to anyone calling her by her full name Linora after she left the Church of Satan.

One day when I asked her why she said "I wanted to leave my name behind with "them" that's what HE (Jay) called me. I always preferred Lin anyway"

Again, I am not a Satanist however I was raised as one. I do not follow any organized religion. I follow the laws of nature & energy. I follow my heart; I follow what Spirit tells me. I worship actual LIGHT and actual DARK, and I worship myself. The actual light and actual dark is our true nature.

My mother

    My pentagram. The one I wear around my neck. It was my mother's, given to her by Anton LaVay. After my parents left the Satanic Church, she put this pentagram away, for her, it held a lot of bad memories including the death of my twin brother. When she passed away, I found it sitting on her dresser, waiting for me. I don't take it off that often. It is my family heirloom. Although a reminder of the destruction of my family, it's a reminder of where I come from and how I still shine coming from the darkest Dark♥

My Mother's Pentagram

Although yes, my mother was a satanic witch, she was many types of a witch. She was also a chaos witch and being as beautiful as she was and knowing it, a sexual deviant as well. She was a mentally and emotionally abusive mother and at times a good mom at times as well.

She would take my sister and I out to the forest and teach us how to look for signs of the faeries as so we could avoid them and not make them angry, and we would leave gifts of silver and cupcakes for them. She would teach us how to listen to the wind in the trees for messages and how to quiet our minds and spirits with the natural elements when we were upset.

She always had the rent paid and food on the table, I never saw her drunk or high, and she was at the bus stop at 5 am every morning going to her hospital job. She was raised Catholic and forced to go to Catholic private school where she was terribly abused and beaten by the nuns there.

We moved when I was in grade 3. My new teacher Mrs. B. was terrible to me, she was super mean. My parents being who they were was well known around the city for their coven parties and the company that they kept and Mrs. B being a Christian woman hated me for it.

Every morning, she had the class say the Lord's prayer and every morning she would make me exit the class and stand in the hallway. She would peer at me over her glasses and shoo her hand at me and then point towards the door. After about a month of this I finally just left the school and walked home (1981 we were independent and had house keys) and I called my mother at work and told her what had been going on. She said she wasn't happy about the imposition of the Lord's prayer being forced on the children and was very sorry that I had been humiliated like that at my new school and she would take care of it. School resumed as usual and moving forward I remained in class during the Lord's Prayer. A few weeks later, over winter break, Mrs. B and her family went to the ski resort and their gondola cable snapped and they all crashed to the ground. It was on the 6 o'clock news and the front page of the news paper. While watching the news report on TV, I looked at my mom, she just looked at me, took a drag off her cigarette, blew out the smoke and said "abracadabra".

Mrs. B suffered multiple broken bones and stayed in the hospital for a long time however no one in her family was killed, everyone eventually recovered. For the rest of the school year, I had a substitute teacher that was very nice to me.

My parents split up in 1978, my mother was having affairs including sleeping with Uncle Jay (I have found romantic notes and pictures from him to her tucked away in the books he had written) and I'm sure what they all did to my brother within the satanic church ultimately destroyed any relationship my parents had. This is undoubtably where the severe hatred my mother had for my father was born. I don't even try to understand her relationship with Jay. You will drive yourself mad trying to make sense out of nonsense. How could she hate my dad and not Jay? The hatred my mother had for my father continued for the rest of their lives. She would spit and curse and say terrible things about my dad, always trying to turn my sister and I against him seething "your precious father!" in such vicious sarcasm every time we said something nice about him. Again, no making sense of my mother and her choices of replacing him with abusive men. I remember the trauma of leaving my home, the day my mom left my dad and we moved into a new house without him, and there was a new man there who I was to start calling Daddy. I instantly rebelled. It was in this new house that I remember at about the age of five being in the basement helping my mom do laundry and suddenly, I was in the corner of the room watching myself and my mom. Knowing now this to be an astral projection, possible trance possession and or I was channeling someone else, (this was the first time I remember it happening however not the last,). I remember hearing and seeing myself call my mom a 'fucking cunt bitch" "whore of Satan" "Devil Fucker" and a "murderer" all while laughing maniacally. I remember watching my mom freaking out and screaming that she hated me and screaming at me to shut up and shaking me and pushing me onto the floor into the pile of laundry, as I watched all of this from across the room, then she ran up the stairs and slammed the door and kept me locked in the basement until my evil stepdad Brian came home.

She wouldn't look at me or talk to me for days. Then everything was okay again, she was right back to calling me her little dolly and baking cookies and being nice to me.

I wasn't alone in the basement; I could feel it. I didn't know it at the time, but I was down there with my other "self" who I didn't get to meet until many years later. I was terrified of the red smiling eyes in the dark corner of the basement staring at me sitting on the steps waiting to be allowed back upstairs. I knew it wasn't Jack.

Over the years I questioned my parents about Jack only to have them change the subject or gaslight me about it every single time. I would ask my dad where was his grave and why didn't he have a grave? My dad would say they didn't keep records of still births back then "or "they didn't bury still births back then". Jack wasn't a stillbirth. I heard him cry. I can still hear him. I remember him crying. There is no birth certificate or death certificate for him, and I have attempted to look up the records and have found nothing about us being born at the hospital.

When I was sent away to England and briefly stayed with my crazy alcoholic aunt, I found a box of letters in the closet. They were from my mother. They were in perfect dated order. I found my birthday. I started to read them. The previously dated letters mother had talked about being pregnant with twins and even had a picture of her boasting about this. Then dated after my birthday saying how both twins had beautiful blue eyes but the girl' eyes were a kind of green blue. And then there was another letter saying that the boy had died a few days later, that something had gone wrong because we were born 6 weeks premature, that she couldn't explain it and she never wanted to talk about him again.

Again, there was never any trace of a birth certificate or a death certificate for my brother. My own birth certificate is dated June 6 (6/6) and states I was born at Vancouver General Hospital. So where was I between May 14 and June 6? I never received an explanation for this.

My mom and her sister, my crazy aunt died six weeks apart. When speaking to my cousin in England after both of our mother's deaths, my aunt's son, I asked him to please look for the box of letters. He said to my dismay that all that type of stuff was thrown away when my aunt was moved into a care home the previous year.

I end this book saying I have no regrets, but not stealing those letters with the picture of my pregnant mother is a huge one. It was the only proof I ever saw of him being here. The picture of mother pregnant with us would be the only picture I would ever have of us together. When I remote view into the womb and see he and I together before our birth, I see us holding pinkies, like a pinky swear, a bonding.

However, the truth about Jack was always in the eyes of my mother. The distant dark deep look.

When I was about 14, after I was harassing her about Jack again, she finally told me how she had scarlet fever when she was born in a bomb shelter in England during the second world war, that the fever had left her unable to have children, medically confirmed sterile, then she came to Vancouver from England having grown up a strict Catholic, and rebelliously met my Dad when she signed up with the church of Satan in 1970.

She said the coven performed a sex conception ritual on the October Full Blood Moon 1972, and she became pregnant with twins, Jack & I.

The Satanic church got Jack, my parents in exchange got me, and in the deal, the daughters of a second-degree Satanic Warlock, my dad, my younger sister, and I, were spared from other ritualistic abuse, we were "off the table" so to speak.

My mother passed away on the October Full Blood Moon 2010.

I had always told her to at least leave the truth written for me somewhere for after her death. When I packed her house up, there was no letter, no mysterious envelope, nothing left for me about Jack anywhere, just her pentagram pendant. When it came time to sell her house after her death, I was taking pictures of the house and property for insurance reasons, and I captured a picture of her ghost at the front door. I have a picture of my own mother's ghost. At least there is that. The resolution of the picture was too poor to include it in this book at this time.

Sometimes I would get mad and demand that my mother tell me what happened to my brother. I put her through hell with it. My dad never saw that side of me, but mother sure did. I would go through bouts of anger and depression and such loneliness, my soul missed him, still misses him and I still wonder how different my life would have been if I had had my brother here on Earth and not just as a spirit. All she would say is "we are vowed to secrecy" as always with a very deep weird look in her eye, start to cry and leave the room. Avoidance. Complete avoidance.

)●(

Throughout my life, when I was younger, I have seen many psychics and mediums and not one has ever brought up my brother. Not one.

Once, while working at a metaphysical shop up north, a popular medium, Jane, was doing psychic readings so I thought I would try her out. She said nothing about Jack. I had not yet become open about my family history; I was still in the satanic closet and didn't come out until I started performing my "Enchanted Evening of the Paranormal" public presentation lectures in 2019, and that was the first time I said it out loud choaking on every word in a room of about 30 people.

I took a deep breath of courage and lightly explained to Jane that my twin brother was murdered at birth by the satanic church and if she could at all pick up on him. She stared at me and then laughed in my face leaving me in complete shock and second guessing my choice to confide in her. She proceeded to tell me that her spirit guide was also laughing at the satanic church and what a bunch of nonsense it was and that I had no twin brother.

I told her she was wrong, and she didn't like that.

I started to see over the next couple years as I worked "the shows", that during open demonstration nights, medium messages nights, when you deliver messages from the dead to the audience members, the mediums would pick the same people over and over in the audience to deliver the same messages from the same dead son, or the same dead husband and on and on. These experiences left me disheartened as I was beginning to see how different I was from everyone else as far as my authenticity went with popularity. I wasn't like the super popular show mediums as I didn't just talk about love and light, I always brought in the truth and the dark along with the light. People don't really like that.

)●(

For me, usually, the strongest connection I have with my client's dead is when they first sit down with me for Tarot or their very first spirit council session and I feel spirit comes through then to establish authenticity with me for them. And I also believe there is only so much to be said from the dead to the living and it is usually a message to confirm that the client is not alone, that their dead loved one is still there, that we do go on and that is comfort that they can hang on to for the rest of their own life left on earth.

It wasn't long before Jane tried to copy my events and other work that I did. One night one of her friends had had a few too many drinks sitting with my then paranormal team at the pub. Me, being sober, always finds this amusing and yes sometimes I use it to my advantage.

This friend was upset with Jane for whatever reason and piped up and said out of the blue "Jane is full of shit" everyone at the table looked at the friend.

Me "oh, how so?" I probably lit up like a comet through space.

Friend "she tells everyone she has been seeing spirits and talking to the dead since she was 4 and that's complete bullshit. I remember her in a psychic development class years ago saying she didn't ever have any communication with the dead, and she wanted to be an actress. She is also copying a dead mentor of mine with her trance and channeling! As soon as my mentor passed away, Jane started using her material!"

Well, well, well. There it was. It's always nice to have conformation in this third dimension we call Earth.

Jane is not the only one out there like this. Although this bothers me immensely, it's not my place to call anyone out and all in all, I have seen the shows make people feel better. Karmic justice will do what it does as always in time.

I meet so many toxic people while working in these metaphysical shops.

Another "healer" at this shop told a regular client of mine that I was weak because I used Tarot cards. Wow, let me clear that right up. I love Tarot cards. However, being one with Tarot now for so long, as the art is a lifetime relationship with your deck, I really don't need the cards anymore. So often I will start delivering the messages as the cards will flash through my mind with messages from my clients guides and I'll be channeling for 15 minutes before I ever flip a card. I never ever get sick of reading Tarot, every time it amazes me and blows my mind! The high I get when I connect with spirits is the best high, I have ever had. Even better is the high when I cross a spirit over to the other side, when they cross, I can only explain it as like my blood turns into 7-up, my blood turns into bubbles, there is nothing else like it.

At one shop, there was mean girl management that recorded, watched, and listened to private readings on a security camera and then made fun of and spread rumors about the clients and would shit talk me behind my back and I now refuse to work my magic at metaphysical shops all together. This is when I started my "Psychic Medium Morals and Ethics" lectures.

I will say this; A true healer will ignite the light within yourself to heal yourself. A true healer will help get your ball rolling and help move stuck traumatic energy so you can care for yourself. A true healer will not have you make weekly or monthly appointments with them. If you find yourself becoming dependent on a healer for your wellbeing, then it is possible that the "healer" is keeping you sick on purpose for capital gain, and they are not in fact a healer but just another form of opportunist. Know your healers and your (Tarot) dealers. Be careful who you let touch you, energy transfer is real. When consulting, you are giving people permission to access you and your energy. For example, every time I read Tarot, my deck absorbs the client's energy, and if the client doesn't remove their energy or permission when the reading is over, I get to keep it. What could I do with it? I can spy on them, check in and see what's going on, I could use it to set up a curse or because I am mostly a good witch, I could send a blessing. Be warned about who you seek council from.

Another psychic medium, who I thought I had become friends with, got together to plan some metaphysical projects and events that we were doing together.

She had proven to me without a doubt over the years that she was authentic! She is an amazing soul and an amazing medium, and I love her very much.

Even though she had given me many messages from my dead friends, she had never brought up my brother either. I thought I would try her out and again I lightly explained my story. I had known her for some time and felt comfortable in doing so. Again, I was being looked at like a deer caught in the headlights. She proceeds to tell me that my mother's spirit was now there with us. My stomach started to turn in disappointment. She continued to say that my mother was explaining that my twin brother had died in childbirth, and it was her guilt of being in the satanic church and performing the blood moon conception ritual that she feared had killed him, not the satanists. My mother was not there. I am very familiar with my mother's ghost, and I still talk to her daily and I knew she was not there. My medium friend was just trying to make me feel better. This same person is the one that stopped working with me because I have the word Occult on my business card. She is very "love and light", and I know the world needs her to be this way. I explained that "Occult" means hidden or mysteries, but some people just can't get past the taboo of the word. My mother would always tell me that I was occult by nature, that the occult was my life path, and she was right.

I would often catch my mother staring at me throughout my life, staring at me like I was a freak-show or paranormal phenomenon, sometimes with fear in her eyes, sometimes with tears and sometimes with love.

My parents and their satanic cult murdered my brother. They killed him. I KNOW IT. I have always known it deep in my soul. My parents never, even at their death ever broke their vows of satanic secrecy. I don't think all satanists are baby killers however just as in any organization, you are going to have good people and bad people.

I can't prove anything. I have tried spells, channeling, seances, astral travel, my spirit council and even Jack won't come through on the subject of my brother. Sometimes I fantasize that he's still here somewhere on Earth, that maybe he's the leader of some Satanic Church or Pagan division cult somewhere. That maybe he might still show up in the flesh one of these days. That my brother and Jack are not the same, because that would mean that there would be a chance my brother was alive somewhere. I know I've missed him here in the 3D, this third dimension we know as life on this planet. I also know, he may not have had a spirit at all, I know that sometimes children come here as theory, as a lesson and he may have been here so I can have this life story.

A few days before my dad died of cancer on Father's Day 2002, he went crazy and frantic and started a bon fire in the back yard burning piles of papers, books and his old ceremonial robe muttering "They can never know! They can never Know!"

My dad's wife Sarah, who was born on Halloween and 20 yrs. younger than my dad, managed to grab a bag of paperwork saving it from the fire and gave it to me after his death. It contains his Satanic Degree Certificate, a rough draft of the original Black Mass, sabbath rituals and hundreds of satanic contacts. Sarah kept a bag containing fake IDs for my dad including fake passports and fake driver's licenses. I have no idea what that was all about, my dad was a man of mystery.

The next day dad was taken into palliative care, and I was sitting with him alone in his hospital room, and he on his death bed. I saw him rise out of himself, like I do in astral. He was standing beside his bed staring at himself laying there in a coma. I said, "Hi daddy" and he turned to look at me and he half smiled I said "you don't have to stay here for us anymore. Your fight is over, you are free". He looked back at himself, and I saw him slowly fade away.

My sister came soon after to spend the night with me in dad's room. Dad was having episodes of talking to his deceased sisters and we could feel their presence in the room like electric energy. We woke up a few hours later to witness him take his last breath and start his journey into the afterlife.

For the next 3 weeks before his funeral, every time I closed my eyes, I had a vision of my dad floating through space. He was wrapped in the hospital blanket, arms crossed on his chest and glowing bright green with his mouth hanging slightly open. It was awful. I didn't understand until much later that this was a partial vision of him in one of the healing centers, afterlife hospitals on the other side where we can rest our soul before moving forward if we need to. I just wasn't getting the whole picture yet.

I now have had my dad's black arts degree framed and on my office wall ever since, and the rest of the sacred texts put away safely. One day, I will own my own Occult School where I can teach about the light, the dark and the arts of witchcraft and within it, my own Occult history museum and have these family heirlooms on display along with all the memorabilia and pictures I have collected on my paranormal investigations. My vision for the Occult school is always present in my mind. A big dark beautiful castle or Victorian mansion. Yes, it will have all the basics, however it will be an advanced school of Occult arts. I will take esoteric education to the next level in an actual school as I offer in private and in lecture classes now.

My dad is partially responsible for my obsession with Occult education and my library. He would give me Occult and witchcraft books for every birthday and sabbat holiday. Once I asked him how I was supposed to remember all this, that so many of the books said different things and have different opinions and perspectives, and he replied that I am not supposed to remember it all. That I would just naturally absorb what was meant for me and that I was meant to create my own magic. That every spell book is like a recipe book and though some recipes are tried and true, that there is always room for modification.

He told me that every book I read is someone else's opinion and I was meant to form my own. That one day I wouldn't need spell books. He often told me I was meant to lead, not to follow. I came to realize as I got older that this was true, and I pass these words of wisdom from my dad to my students.

Each step, in every ritual, is to build up your frame of mind, your vibration, to achieve your goal through manifestation of the power of your will. I love the romance of rituals and still use them when casting for students or a group for their benefit, however I don't need to do it anymore. I noticed a long time ago that I get what I want just by thinking about it, good and bad. The power of our mind and will is incredible. And to add, after the death of both my parents, I get whatever I want.

I always knew I would wait until my parent's deaths before I told my story. I did not want my parents to suffer murder charges and relive the trauma. They were my parents, and I loved them. I still love them.

My dad, knowing I was incredibly psychic, gave me my Tarot deck for my 11th Birthday. It was my destiny.

Me, 1992 photo shoot for a Pagan magazine

It is very important to me to continue to teach traditional Tarot, as it is getting lost in the New Age times of Oracle Decks and "versions" of Tarot. I realized that I myself had never had a Tarot reading. I would go for a Tarot reading and the reader would have oracle cards or put a few Tarot cards on the table and start giving me advice. To me, Tarot is so much more than that. Tarot, real true-blue Tarot, is my calling. I have dedicated much of my life to studying the old ways of reading and putting together the craft of the cards. It is so much a part of me now, in my blood and my DNA. Spirit will just flash me a Tarot card in my mind if I'm needed to know something quickly, its an even faster understanding than Jack telling me something sometimes, or maybe it is Jack (or Rebecka who you will meet shortly) flipping a card at me.

Looking back at my psychic progression is an amazing thing that I use to help my students. There always was a little voice in my head, to the right of me, whispering secrets and detailed information in my right ear when reading Tarot. I thought it was just invasive spirit clutter and always ignored it. As the years went on, the voice got louder. It wasn't Jack. It was a woman's voice. For a long time, I thought it might be Brandi, my childhood friend who is now deceased, but it turns out its Rebecka.

I finally met Rebecka when I put myself into an intention trance to finally figure out who belonged to this voice I had been hearing since I first shuffled Tarot all those years ago. I sat in my chair at the grand fireplace with 2 huge stone Gargoyles on either side in my castle's main receiving wing. This is where I go in the 5th dimension to meet other spirit council members besides Jack. I sat there, waiting for her to show up and sit down in the vacant grand chair across from me. Instead, she showed up as she always does, beside me on the right.

I said "hi, who are you?"

She said, "I am Rebecka, the spirit of your Tarot, or your Tarot spirit guide if you will."

I knew it! I knew her name was Rebecka the whole time. I always had that name stuck in my head.

Me "come sit down with me."

Rebecka appeared in the chair across from me.

She had long wavy dark red hair, very pale skin and her eyes were green just like mine. She was dressed all in black, just like I do. Clearly, she was Celtic. I could feel the history between us, beyond this life.

I said "we have known each other a long time

Rebecka"

Rebecka "Yes"

Me "thank you for all your help with Tarot "

Rebecka "No thanks needed. It what we do. It is what you and I do. It is what we have always done."

Me "well accept my gratitude just the same."

Rebecka "of course"

Then the vision ended, I came out of trance. Now, especially when working big psychic fairs or conventions, I say, "c'mon Becky, time to go to work!" and we go to work. I can go and go and go for hours reading Tarot! I believe my record so far is 25 flash event style readings in 4 hrs and I can tell you I have help from Rebecka. It takes a lot of energy to raise my vibration to meet spirit and read Tarot as reading Tarot is not just the meaning of the cards, it is also spirit communication that comes with it.

I have energetic surges when reading Tarot and when being creative in my projects. When the downloading starts, it doesn't stop until it stops. When reading Tarot, my vibration elevates, and not only can I talk to Jack & Becks, but I can talk to my client's dead too, sometimes. I never promise mediumship, it just happens. Quite often an unfortunate side effect of this vibration is men think they have fallen in love with me. So many times, I will get a message from a male client shortly after I have read for them telling me that they can't stop thinking about me and that they think they are in love with me. I quickly explain that they are not in love with me, and it is indeed a side effect of the Tarot reading or spiritual service they received and that their feelings for me will go away. Most of the time this works, and their emotions calm down and they get used to vibe when they see me a few more times, but not always. I have also lost clients and students who just can't get past it. It turns into a problem, sometimes even a stalker problem.

I was reading tarot for 25 years before I realized, before I trusted that I was practicing mediumship with Tarot. I don't know why as I have been seeing and talking to the dead my whole life. I guess I just had it in my head that it was separate. A limited belief. I signed up for a live crash course in mediumship about a decade ago. As soon as I met the facilitator, Lynne, I knew we were going to be friends and we still are! Lynne said to me in the first class "why are you here? You are a medium already."

Me" I know but I want to advance."

Lynne "You need to trust. You know that little voice in your head when you read Tarot? That's spirits, that's mediumship. That's how you receive" I now know that its mostly Rebecka when I am reading Tarot. Other peoples spirit guides and Jack are different, and I can definitely feel the difference.

Trust. Trust the little voice in my head.

So, the next day I had a client sit across from me as always. While I'm shuffling the cards, I see a little old man with a big smile standing behind her waving at me. Not the first-time seeing spirits during readings, just the first time I'm not going to ignore them.

Me, sounding lame and cliché "I believe I have your dad here with us."

Client "ok wow!"

Then my mind is filled with pictures of shiny new pots and pans. I always thought of these visions as daydreams or nonsense, imagination garbage. As clutter that would get in the way of my reading Tarot.

In my mind I hear Lynne say "trust"

Me, here goes nothing, "your dad is showing me pictures of shiny new pots and pans."

Well, the client lost it and started crying "the last birthday present my dad gave me before he died was my dream set of pots and pans!"

My readings were never the same after that. Now it is not uncommon to start downloading messages from the dead the second the client makes the appointment with me. I see and hear the dead all the time, everywhere, and now I incorporate it into my Tarot readings too. All kinds of people cry during Tarot readings, sometimes even after only 2 cards down. I must explain that this is normal, that they are experiencing high vibration. It is especially impressive when it is the big tough guys or skeptics that start to cry. I get very excited as I know it is life changing for them as it confirms spiritual connection.

Lynne and I started to teach psychic development classes together and she joined me as a partner in my local paranormal investigations becoming a well renowned local Paranormal Investigation Team.

With the both of us being legit psychic mediums, we have had great success with our Steveston Ghost Walks, in our hometown mostly all year round, not just in the spooky Fall. One night while teaching Psychic Development classes together, Lynne stopped in the middle of class and proclaimed "Ok, that is the third time this spirit has walked through our circle interrupting me. I am going to talk to him, I'm going to ask him who he is and why he is here." When spirits show up in a group setting like this, it is common for the spirit to be related to or be a friend of one of the living people that are there. Lynne relays that this spirit's name is Kabooga or Kabowa or something like that. He was a fisherman here in Steveston back in the 1960's and passed away in the late 1970's from liver problems. He is not happy with all the construction that is taking place in the village and wants us to know that." This spirit then left our classroom and we carried on with class. After class I went home and told my husband about this ghost who showed up in our psychic development class mentioning the odd name of Kabooga and to my surprise, my husband said that name sounded very familiar and proceeded to call his mother to ask her about the name. His mother immediately confirmed that "Kaboogie" was the village bootlegger back in the day who happened to live directly behind where our psychic development classes were being held and how her brother had gone out fishing with him back in 1965. Right after that phone call, my husband called his uncle who confirmed that yes, Kaboogie was Harry Watson who had died from alcoholism in the late 1970's. And that's how the Steveston Ghost walks were born. We have collected ghost stories from the old Maritimers, the Steveston archives and many of our experiences during paranormal investigations and have put together an amazing ghost walking tour of deaths, murder, and mayhem in our sleepy seaside village of Steveston. One of the most famous stories is about our very own axe murderer Yip Luk and the beheading of our town police officer who's spirits still walk the streets of Steveston today.

Lynne and I have conducted countless classes, psychic fairs, paranormal investigations at private residences and famous locations, seances and seminars and everything spooky under the moon together. It is quite amazing how much fun we have and how well we work together.

Lynne always takes the best pictures of me.

JACK

H E'S ALWAYS BEEN THERE. I DON'T remember him not being there. Sometimes my shadow, sometimes my light. Sometimes he's in front of me, beside me or behind me, but he's always there. He protects me sometimes to a fault as I know bad things happen to people that do me wrong. Sometimes I just see him and other times its just his voice telling me things. He still guides me through decision making by saying "No!" like I'm a puppy about to eat a shoe with such a forceful energy almost like when the driver of a car uses their arm as your seatbelt when stopping suddenly. It feels like a huge heavy blanket being draped over me sometimes, "NO!" It was years before I saw Jack's full body. He's always there, he's as much a part of me as my myself. He is beautiful to look at. Almost 6 feet tall, black as black wavy hair and the darkest bluest eyes. Like my dad's eyes. His facial features are sharp and rugged. Jack also has a horse who is exactly half black and half white right down the middle with the blue eye being on the black side and the dark eye being on the white side He shows himself to me as a gunslinger, all in black, sometimes he has a huge black male wolf with him, who I've named Tarot. Jack says Tarot, the wolf, is also mine. They together, are my protection. When I was about 5 or 6, I had a vision of a black wolf pup. I found him in the forest, and I knew his mother wolf couldn't take care of him and she had left him there for me. When I bent down to pick up the baby wolf, I saw my long silver hair reach the ground, and silver rings on my fingers. I was an older woman.

I have long silver hair now, so I imagine the wolf isn't too far off in my future.

Jack tells me everything. When I get mad at Jack for not telling me things such as warnings with his heavy "NO's", he says that's on me. I planned these lessons for myself before I came to Earth so I can be the powerful dark worker that I am, so I can bring the light. When teaching psychic development, one of the first things taught is how to meet your spirit guides. Its like basic psychic development 101. Well, one night in class circle, a student started to describe Jack. Then another, and then another! Jack was having fun with me. He was being playful bouncing around my students. Maybe he was trying to make me jealous I don't know, he just laughed at me. Soon after that incident, Jack showed up and sat down across from me while I was reading a book on the couch. He didn't look calm and cool like he usually did, he looked annoyed and like something was bothering him. It never occurred to me that Jack might have problems and need to talk! So, I asked him "what is wrong with you?" he waved his hand and suddenly, I saw what I can only describe as a beautiful blonde fairy type of young woman tethered to him fluttering about all around him in excitement. I looked at Jack to explain and all he said was "I was assigned an apprentice" and I laughed at him and said "you what?! You have spirit guide apprenticeships over there? That's cool" Jack smiled and left me to my book.

NECROMANCY

I REMEMBER MY FIRST EXPERIENCE WITH NECROMANCY. I was about 7 years old, and my sister was 5. We had rabbits in our yard and one morning my sister and I found 4 dead baby bunnies all torn apart with their insides strewn about. We were devastated. It just seemed natural to us to draw a circle around them and a star, a pentagram, for each one. I found a stick and we did our best to put the organs back inside the little rabbits. We held hands and we wished as hard as we could for them to come back to life and when they didn't, we ran crying to our mother. We showed her what was wrong and initially she thought we had sacrificed the rabbits with the circle and pentagrams. She stated in horror "Oh my god, did you girls do this?!" and thinking she meant the circle and putting their insides back in we said "Yes" Ill never forget the look on her face, so funny now. She said with absolute fury "why would you hurt these baby rabbits?!! What were girls trying to do?!" and of course I cleared that up by telling her they were dead already, and we were trying to bring them back to life. She then looked so proud of us and tried to comfort us, and we had a little funeral for the bunnies.

Being a mortician, a postmortem surgeon, it is common for me to get murder victims and unsolved murder victims, I'm not going to lie, I've tried to receive information from them about what happened, for the greater good of course. I've done necromancy spells to find out what happened to them, to retrieve information from the body as mediumship, talking to the spirit, is not always available as the spirit is usually already in transition and "busy". I always, if permitted and feel that they may be open to it, offer this to the families that I serve. Sometimes it works, and sometimes it doesn't. I feel that is that way as some information is not to be known. You can be the most powerful of a witch however if the Gatekeepers don't permit you knowing the information requested, you are not going to get your answers. This is where we need to let go and trust that things unfold as they should. You may not get the answers you need now, but one day, if on this planet or in the afterlife, you will.

When I was about the same age around the time of the necromancy bunnies, I had an experience of being struck by a white lightening bolt through my bedroom window as I lay in bed. I remember it was still dark out, the morning light was starting to show itself. Suddenly ZAP. I can only describe it as forked white lightening. I realize that if it had been lightening as we know it, the glass of my window would have been shattered. It was a kind of energy lightning. It hit me so hard that it knocked the wind out of me, and I was unable to move or scream, and a moment later my mother came into my room and put some clothes away into my dresser and as hard as I tried, I could not breathe or scream or move and she left. I eventually came out of it and went looking for my mother and found her down in the laundry room where I had my "episode" some time before, so I waited for her at the top of the stairs and she told me that it had just been a bad dream, but I knew it wasn't.

I had two more incidents with lightning as I got older, making it three in my life so far. The second time was driving through the valley through a terrible nighttime rainstorm. ZAP! The car was struck by lightening almost making us crash. I could taste the electricity in my mouth for days. And the third time, I was living up north in a lake house I owned with my rockstar boyfriend at the time. I could hear the storm coming, the beautiful thunder rumbling so I went to sit on the porch to watch it come in. The house sat on the edge of the lake on the edge of the forest. Before my eyes I see them! Two very large white wispy ghosts fly by through the trees in front of me and in that fraction of that second BANG! Our house was struck by lightening. It took out the power and all the appliances and left a huge burn streak on the side of the house. After the mayhem of it all, I had time to reflect on the two white ghosts that I saw. They were forest spirits getting out of the way of the lightening.

I often wondered if the lightening zap I suffered in my bed as a child was an alien abduction. Theres no way to really tell. At the age of four, I recall playing in the living room on the second floor of our house on a rainy day. And I looked up and out of the wide-open curtains through our large living room window and saw a huge spaceship. I mean it was massive. It looked like a classic UFO, and it wasn't making any noise, it was silent and then it moved out of view and couldn't be seen anymore. I remember the phone ringing and my mother quickly running to the window saying to the neighbor on the phone that she couldn't see anything. My mom looked at me and I said, "I saw it" and the color washed out of her face when I said "spaceship" because that was obviously what the neighbor had told her, and I couldn't hear what they were talking about. Here we are over 40 years later and someone on a hometown Facebook page is asking if anyone else saw this incident between 1977 – 1978. Wow.

Fast forwarding to about 2008 my friend Leslie and I were on a road trip from Prince George to Vancouver. We woke up in my car on the side of the road in the middle of the night with 8 hours missing. Our bodies hurt like we had been beaten up; we were so sore and so hungry and thirsty. The last thing we both remember was driving in daylight through the valley. We still have no explanation for this missing time, we are pretty sure it was an alien abduction.

LEARNING THE DARK

My first crush at 5 years old was Darth Vader. I remember seeing him on the big screen at the theater and it was the first time I felt my heart move for a boy. My second crush was Anubis when studying Egypt in grade 5. I grew into the teenage daughter from hell. Satan is my ultimate mythical creature fantasy bad boy. I was a terrible kid. Boys, motorbikes, drugs galore and party, party, party. I was so lucky and never suffered with any addictions. Being an addict wasn't in my cards. I just suffered with everyone else's addictions as time went on. I was dealing hash and LSD at 14 and was even arrested and handcuffed at my desk in grade 9 math class at the school for bad kids for selling weed, yes handcuffed at my desk! I was arrested for church vandalism and church arson all before I was 15. I didn't set the church on fire, my dear friend Vladdy did, I was just there, just as guilty. Lucky, it was in my cards to not have a criminal record and I am clean as whistle as an adult. I eventually smartened up. The first time I attempted suicide I cut my wrists when I was 12. I just didn't want to be here anymore. I knew I didn't belong and just wanted to go "home". I wanted to follow the voice of the partially invisible boy at the time who felt like home. Jack.

Along with this teenage rebellion came juvenile delinquent boys who did time in juvie jail. I met James when he was released from juvie through my best friend and closest thing I had to an actual flesh brother, Vladdy who I mentioned earlier, who unfortunately died from cancer in 2019. There was an instant connection between James and me. I was 15 and he was 17. Before long he was sneaking me into his house in the middle of the night and we would indulge in teenage lust and practice witchcraft.

His mother was also a satanic witch. One night as we were laying in his bed, we heard his mother chanting, and it was getting louder and louder, maybe in Latin. We snuck down the hallway and looked through the door into the den at the end of the hall to see his mother siting there naked in front of candles and books. Then we both saw it. A huge black mass rise above from behind her. She started to scream the foreign words louder and louder then grabbed a knife and took it to her throat! We were in shock! James ran in and got the knife away from her and I ran back into his room to hide, and he got me out of there in before the ambulance and the cops showed up.

Unfortunately, that wasn't the last time something like that happened to James. The next time, his mother had grabbed an axe and attacked him with it during one of her ritual episodes. He was in his room listening to music on his Walkman and his mother just burst into his room in a frenzy swinging the axe at him. He was not hurt in the incident, just traumatized. I will never forget seeing that black mass rise from the corner, never. His mother died from alcoholism on December 25th, 2005.

James and I were lovers and friends through out our adult life as well, he was one of the best friends I've ever had, until he was killed drinking and driving in 2006. He smashed his car into a telephone pole during a rainstorm heading home from the bar.

It was one night when I was about 23 that James and I were hanging out that he told me I needed to write a book. And after he said it, he looked at me seriously and said, "you know Ill always be there for you baby". To this day I hear his voice say those words when I need to hear them.

As an adult, James started to wear this terrible cologne, I still don't know what it was. One day while at work, I could suddenly smell this awful man perfume and stopped everything I was doing to look around for my friend because he was the only one I knew that wore that stuff. There was no one there, so I though it to be a sign to give him a call to see how he was, it had been a few months since I talked to him, to which he didn't answer, and he didn't call me back.

Two weeks later I heard the terrible news that he was killed on that day I smelled his cologne. James had come to say goodbye. I dream about him all the time. In my dreams, he is always still alive somewhere. He has always faked his death. I believe I dream this because I never got to say goodbye, I never saw his body, his funeral was kept private and I lived far away from him at that time.

My mom sent me away to England when I was 15 to live with my crazy aunt to straighten me up. As soon as I stepped off the plane and was able to breathe the air, I knew I had been there before. I found out later that my parents had moved me to England for six months right after I was born. Gee I wonder why? Something to do with the trauma they had put themselves through with the satanic church, I am sure. This was where and when I found the letters about my mother's pregnancy. I ran away from my aunts after my 16th birthday because she was a drunk and there was a dark entity in the room that I had to stay in at her house. From there, I back packed across England and lived like a Vagabond for 7 months until the authorities caught me sleeping in a beautiful, abandoned church in Rockingham, took me to the Canadian Embassy in London and deported me back to Vancouver.

During the daytime, the spirits in that old church told me and taught me all kinds of things about colors. Ever since my time with them I can see auras on people and on trees. It wasn't long before I noticed I could see death on people as well, illness and cancer. At night, they showed me visions, like movies about medieval villages and wars. The style of the visions, I recognize them now as visions, I receive when I am downloading information from spirit. It is a lot like daydreaming, but different.

I've had an abnormally high number of friends die from drugs, alcohol, and accidents. Having my dead twin brother beside me in spirit, I was obsessed with death growing up, and not to mention my mother had me believe I had killed a sexual predator at the age of 9 which I will get to shortly.

When I was 18, my dear friend Dan ,29, was killed in a terrible drinking and driving car accident on the old Hope – Princeton highway coming home from the Penticton Peach festival. His sister Steph and I had to identify his body in a hospital morgue way out of town. This was my first friend to die and my first trip to the morgue.

When they pulled the sheet down off his face for us to identify him, he still looked like himself, maybe like he had been in a bar fight. 10 days later, at his viewing, after his embalming and before his funeral he looked terrible, not like himself at all. I looked at his body, at his face caked in makeup and I thought "I could have done a way better job" and that's when the seeds for my funeral director and mortuary career were planted.

Dan has remained with me; he shows up every now and then here and in astral. Always the same, always with a beer in his hand and a gleam in his eye. Its always good to see him and he always has something to tell me.

My bestie growing up, Brandi, was captured into the life of drugs and ended up on the downtown East side in our mid 20's after suffering severe childhood trauma. We went through a lot together so very young. I first met Brandi when we were 7, in the mean Mrs. B's class. Brandi was my first friend at that new school and had showed me compassion for being made to sit in the hallway every morning during the Lord's prayer. She unfortunately eventually succumbed to AIDS. I see her all the time in astral, all the time. She visits me at least twice a month. Sometimes she's happy, sometimes she's not, and when she is not, we are sitting in her childhood home. She tells me she has lots to do on the other side, lots of jobs and that she is an ambassador of sorts. She knows she messed up her life and that the 3rd dimension still haunts her sometimes.

When my friend Denise died of her body rejecting a double lung transplant due to her cystic fibrosis, I was living up north and didn't get to visit her in time before she died. I was very upset about this. Denise was a lot of fun and we had good times together. After I had been attacked and stabbed at a party one night, it was Denise who sat with me in the hospital for 2 days holding my good hand to comfort me. The very next night after she died, I had a visitation with her spirit. I realized I was in a hospital hallway; I saw her name on the outside of the door, and I knew I was in astral, and I was going to get to see her. I walked into her room, and she was sitting on the bed. She looked happy and so beautiful. I sat down beside her, and we held hands once again. There was a big open window before us, and the morning sun was softly beaming in and the curtains lightly blowing in the breeze. We just smiled at each other, and she let go of my hand and then she just floated out the window into the light. I'm still running high emotions writing about this experience all these years later.

And then there was Frank. Frank was an amazing friend to both me and my sister. He was always there to help us out. He gave both my sister and I a set of keys to his apartment in Kitsilano just in case we ever needed somewhere to go. That year of his death, I was surprising him with Nine Inch Nails concert tickets for his birthday that very night. He was a pilot, and I knew he was on Vancouver Island selling his old plane to buy himself a new one for his birthday and he was going to call me at about 3pm. I didn't hear from him, and I called and called and there was no answer. I was getting a sick feeling in my stomach, and I knew something was wrong. A friend called me at about 6pm and told me to quickly put on the news, something terrible had happened. There on the TV screen was Frank's float plane nose dived into the beach and the news reporter was talking about no survivors. His plane had stalled coming into the bay. There were 2 grade six classes learning how to kayak right where he needed to emergency land. He had to make a decision.

I can see it as if I was right there beside him flying the plane. I could feel his anxiety, I could hear the wind and I could hear him take a deep breath and say "fuck" as the plane was going down.

He killed himself and the 2 people who were going to buy his plane. It was either the kids kayaking in the bay or them. He was on the front page of the news paper the next day labeled as a hero. He died on his 34th birthday. His death was the first time I projected myself through time to see an event. My sister and I still suffer his loss. He is dearly missed. He is the only one I know who has died on his birthday and in a plane crash.

Ricky was my first addict friend. We met 1986 in grade 8. We were 13. Ricky had long ginger red hair and we became fast friends and remained friends through high school and as adults. We both started going grey together at 15 years old, for very different reasons. My grey hair was hereditary, and Ricky's was from stress. Ricky was my mom's favorite of all my friends. She absolutely adored him and wasn't shy about letting my other friends know that he was her favorite. I would come home from wherever and he would be there at my house having tea, being fed, and playing cards or watching TV with my mom, just hanging out. Unfortunately, Ricky started using needles and heroin by the time he was 14 and it was a battle with him his whole life.

This is where I learned that no amount of witchcraft or magic can save someone if they are not willing to give up what makes them sick in the first place. I really tried everything in my witch's toolbox to save him from addiction when we were younger. He had time where he was good and cleaned right up and then he would fall, up and down his whole life. It truly was a constant battle.

During his last coma, I went to go say goodbye, we all thought he wasn't coming back from this one. But he did. He came out of it. He said he remembered all kinds of weird stuff from his coma that he would share with me to use in my paranormal research when he was feeling better.

He soon after passed away from an overdose in 2023 before I had the chance to talk to him again. His death hit me hard even though had anticipated it for nearly 40 years. However, I did talk to him after death. He came to visit me about a month later. He was happy and looked great. We hugged and cried, he went on to tell me some incredible things, including all about his afterlife rehab center. He told me that it took 3 weeks to detox earth and the drugs from his spirit. He told me, that the detox program on the other side used way better drugs than anything he ever used on earth and without withdrawal or any side effects when he was done. He went into detail about choices that we make and how I can use this information to help other spirits that are trapped on earth because of their attachments to earth drugs. And he is right.

Over the last 10 years or so, there are more earth-bound spirits than ever because of all the fentanyl overdoses. I have experienced that they do not want to cross over because they want to remain close to their addiction. Now, I tell them about Ricky. And now, 2/3 of them go to cross over. It is amazing. Thank you, Ricky.

Halloween, Samhain, is my favorite sabbat and I go all out to honor to my dead. Besides the empty seated full placement honorary dinner table, carved jacks and all the things that make a meaningful Halloween Sabbat, I now turn my front yard into a cemetery and have all my friends and my parents "buried" out there with their own personalized headstones and everything. It is very meaningful to me and a very harsh reality.

I am now a fully licensed, although slowly retiring, Funeral Director, Mortician and Embalmer specializing in sever trauma repair and restoration. I am certified in crematorium operations; I am a certified Master of Funeral Ceremony officiant specializing in Pagan death ritual rites. Now, my mortuary career is going to be another book for sure. The stories I have about the toxic corporate hazing through my mortuary apprenticeship and being a psychic medium funeral director are brutal…. I've seen some stuff in my career that started in 2004 when I started embalming under the table without a license in hopes of getting an apprenticeship back then. There is the story of the barnacle man who had been lost at sea for over a year, the skeleton boy and his eagles, the maggot man, the dancing dead fetus and so many more whose stories I want to write in remembrance and respect.

Let me say, funeral homes are for the living. Very rarely did I see human spirits at the funeral home. It was the places I picked the bodies up from that were haunted.

The bodies that came from Vancouver General Hospital's morgue had a unique stench to them, they smelled different than other morgue bodies.

I was not the only one that noticed this, everyone knew by the smell of the body bag if it had come in from VGH without even looking at the paperwork. By the time I legally started funeral service, I was already a very experienced paranormal investigator. I have spent time and conducted paranormal investigations for over 25years in some pretty notorious places ; Salem Massachusetts, New Orleans, Denver Colorado including Croke -Patterson Mansion, Cheeseman Park and The Overlook/ Stanley Hotel, Las Vegas, Bangor Maine, Manresa Castle Port Townsend Washington, Myrtles Plantation House in Louisiana, numerous famous haunts around Vancouver BC, Vancouver Island and British Columbia including creating and hosting The Steveston Ghost Walks in my home town for years now, and countless, cemeteries everywhere I go. I communicate with and have crossed spirits over for many years now for private clients. I can change the directions of portals to relieve homes of orb traffic. I know how to see and what to look for when it comes to spirits, human and nonhuman. I am experienced in paranormal phenomena.

I knew the smell on the VGH bodies was nonhuman.

At one point in time, the transportation service my funeral home was using to transfer bodies to us was on strike. I was assigned to do the pick ups from the VGH morgue. The first thing I noticed as I walked into the morgue is "the smell", so familiar. Then, I walked by the open wide windows of the autopsy room that look like a butcher shop with butchers butchering fresh and old corpses. Then the big steel doors that open to a massive crypt, and once fully inside the crypt, that distinct unique smell almost blew me over. There were bodies on stretchers for ¼ mile. Some in body bags and some not. Some bodies were stacked on shelves off to the side and up the walls.

As the crypt got deeper, it became darker and darker towards the far back of this room of stanching death. Flickering lights and everything. Then I saw it. It was the biggest black shadow mass I've ever seen. It was at lest 100 times bigger than the one at James' place that night. It slowly moved from the furthest back right upper corner of the morgue down the wall and under some stretchers on the left. This was the smell. It belonged to this shadow.

Over time I must have seen it about a dozen times, in different spots in this morgue. And when I asked Jack what it was, he said "it was a collection of residual energy that death can sometimes have, and now it just "lives" there, it always will."

I took charge of the body donation program through the funeral home and had to visit VGH often to pick up torsos, and other dismembered body parts used for medical practices. Although these body parts were kept in a different refrigeration location, I could always smell the shadow when I went there. On one occasion, I had to pick up 7 severed heads. And I could smell the shadow entity so very strongly on them. It was obvious that the shadow visited these other parts of the hospital.

Dead is dead; however, the bodies do tell stories. Some bodies I would look at and I would know by the condition they were in that they were happy they were dead; their suffering was over. And sometimes I wondered if their suffering had just begun.

A deceased man about 30 years old was assigned to me at the funeral home. He had completed suicide after getting in an argument with his wife who I had previously made his funeral arrangements with. I often meet with the families of the deceased before the bodies come in, before I get the medical examiners report before I can create the death certificates. I asked her how he had completed suicide and she said he had cut his wrists. No mention of anything else. His body came into the morgue a few days later.

It's always a mystery before you open the body bag, you never really know what you are going to find in them. I opened his body bag to witness the saddest expression of pain and torment frozen on this man's face. I had never seen anything like it, I still haven't seen anything like it again. Being a psychic medium kicked in and I could still feel his torment. It was extremely uncomfortable for me. Then I turn off the psychic abilities and I see the damage to his body! This man not only cut both his wrists to the point of almost dismemberment, but he had also stabbed himself in the chest 7 times! Emergency surgeons tried to save his life, there was still scissors and clamps holding his chest open and a piece of his rib cage hanging from them trying to patch up his heart from the fatal knife wound. It was brutal. That man's face haunted me because I knew he was still not at peace. I could feel his spirit was still being tortured. I could not get that look off his face. I was upset because it was my job to get that look off his face and I could not. I have so many morgue stories.

SHINE ON, YOU CRAZY DIAMOND

Being a candle is not easy. In order to give light, one must first burn.

O H, THE TERRIBLE THINGS THAT NOTICE you when you SHINE.

When I was 9, my mom thought she would have an old friend from England watch us before school since she left between 4 and 5am to go work at the hospital. This man was an older man. He played the accordion and had long yellow teeth and always wore a brown tartan suit. One morning before school and obviously after my mother had left for work, I felt him get into bed with me and start to put his hand down the back of my jammies.

I heard Jack say "run!" but what I did was grab my lamp from the bedside table and smash him in the head with it. I remember blood splattered on the wall. I remember grabbing my little sister out of her bed and running out of the house to the neighbors who called the police.

I remember the cop car ride to the hospital where I was given a light examination to make sure the blood on me was not mine and I was interviewed by a social worker. I remember my mom and her asshole boyfriend picking us up hours later. I remember when we got home, the blood on the wall had been cleaned up and my mom told me that I had killed the babysitter with the lamp, and that he had died in the hospital from the head injury and that I wouldn't have to worry about him anymore. Fast forward to the age of 17 and I run into this dead man, alive and well at the mall! I remember looking at him as if I was looking at his ghost. I asked my friend if they could see him too and they did! We followed him around the mall for a while until he got into his car and left. When I got home, I asked my mom what the hell?! And she said she didn't want me worrying about him when I was a kid. My Mother let me think I killed someone my whole childhood.

I believe this childhood trauma and the constant beatings and abuse from my stepdad caused me to act out and be mean to other kids at school. Now I had the stigma of Witch parents and I had accidently killed someone attached to me. No one liked me and I was angry and became a bully. I acted out.

MY MOM'S ASSHOLE BOYFRIEND BRIAN

He was always mean to me however started beating me at 7yrs old. When my mom left my dad that horrible day that I can still clearly remember when I was 4, I soon turned 5 and we moved in with Brian shortly after and I did not like him, I wanted my dad. The first time I felt rage, hate and wanting pure revenge and wished death on someone was because of him towards him. He threatened me that if I told my dad about the abuse, that he would kill my little sister, who he didn't beat on, and that he would shoot my dad.

I was forced to call this monster my dad and had to call my real daddy "uncle" in his presence if I was to bring him up at all and only if I absolutely had too. This was when my feelings for my mother started to change to a noticeable anger. Maybe this was when the little demon me from the laundry room incident was born.

Finally, after years of living like that in pure emotional and physical hell, when I was 12 after a particularly bad beating over getting caught stealing my mom's cigarettes, I called and told my dad. I called him and told him that Brian had been beating me. And although my dad had always asked me over the years if I was Ok, I lied to my dad and many other people who had asked about bruises and my bad moods and rages to protect him and my sister.

I remember a few hours later after the phone call to my dad, after dinner time, there was a knock on the door, and I was surprised to see my dad. My mom let him in, she was surprised and concerned. My Dad pulled out his wallet and gave me a $20 and told my sister and I to go the candy store up the road. I remember seeing My mom, Dad and Brian sitting at the kitchen table when I closed the door to go to the store. I remember walking back from the store and seeing 3 cop cars speed by us, sirens and lights and everything and I heard Jack say, "don't worry, your dad took care of Brian". We ran the rest of the way home to find the cop cars at our house, the kitchen was trashed, my mom was crying, and my dad was taken away in the cop car with a big smile on his face. We never saw Brian again.

The violent interactions with men continued.

I had an attempted kidnapping when I was 15. I was way too young to be at this house party. An adult man decided he "wanted" me and when everyone was busy watching the live band, he pushed me down the stairs and kicked my ribs in, broke them all, so I couldn't run away. He picked me up and opened the front door of the house to take me away only to find the cops responding to a noise complaint. I freaked out, he through my broken body at the cops and I fell on the ground and the cops arrested him and I went to the hospital for a few days. My ribs still plague me to this day.

Once again, when I was 20, a 42yr old man picked me out at the bar one night and followed me back to an after-bar house party. On the way to the house party, my best friend threw up on me in the cab on route, so I arrived at the party covered in her vomit. My friend Rod lived next door to the party and Rod said I could borrow some clothes and gave me his house keys to go clean up. This 42 yr. old monster followed me to Rod's house and trapped me inside. He and a 16yr old girl, both complete strangers to me at this time, were wasted on crystal meth, (I found out details later) and the monster man started to severely beat me while preaching the bible. He held me down and at gun point, and had this girl stab me 3 times. She was instructed by him to stab my eyes out and because of all the blood from the beating, my hand slipped and caught the knife saving my eye. The knife went through my hand causing a severe injury. The whole time, I heard and saw a shadow spirit flying around the room laughing. This drug addict man had me trapped for almost an hour, and just when he was going to rape me, the room was flooded with police car lights and the bad guys ran away. Again, I was taken to the hospital, a long recovery after my injuries. This is where Denise sat with me for 2 days holding my good hand. The police and friends informed me who these attackers were and their details. I went into a dark place for about a year after that. I put the word out that I would marry who ever brought me their heads, no one did. My dad said his friend went to take care of them and was told to get in line. Apparently, this monster had a lot of enemies, and I was lucky to get away with I did.

Not too much later in life I met my friend and sometimes house mate, Xave, who was like a brother to me. He told me that the monster drug addict man was his foster dad early in life and had abused him terribly when he was a very young teen. We had this monster in common.

About 10yrs after my attack, I heard Xave's Harley pull into my driveway, it wasn't uncommon for him to visit and have tea and I would read his Tarot. He came inside, and I saw Jack in the living room looking at me like "oh wow" so I knew this wasn't an ordinary visit. We sat at the kitchen table, and

Xave looked at me, he was quite dreamy looking back in the day, dark curly black hair and deep blue eyes, kind of like Jack.

I said to him "so, what's up?"

He looked at me and said, "he's dead."

I responded, "please don't tell me it was a car crash." It would have been too easy of a death.

Xave said, "he was killed in jail 10 days ago. Stabbed to death."

We shared the moment and then I told him what happened to me about 10 nights ago.

Well,10 nights ago, the night the monster was killed, I had one of my out of body episodes. I was dragged out of my bed and pulled down the hall going to somewhere very bad. I was scared and I wasn't alone. I saw other people being pulled too. I know now that this was Monster trying to drag everyone that he's harmed to his doomed afterlife with him.

Wait, there's more; Exactly 25 years later, on the exact 25yr anniversary of my attack, I went into work at the funeral home, and I saw, I recognized, the then 16-year-old girl, the co attackers name, on our intake board in the office. I can't even describe the waves of every emotion that I felt in that second. "No way". I calmly walked into the morgue and opened her body bag to see the remains of a street working drug addict hooker with AIDS that died from a fentanyl overdose. I processed her body. I did it with care and grace like I would anyone else. I felt pity for her now, imagining what the monster must have done to her to make her be the way she was the night of my attack and for her to be like this now.

EVEN LOVERS

I WAS A DEEP ROMANTIC. I'VE HAD many lovers. Some of them good, and some of them bad.

I had a warning with this one that I completely ignored. One night while hanging out at the very beginning of the romance, he had turned around and his face had morphed into my evil stepdad Brian from childhood. It almost knocked me off my chair.

This was the first time I had seen "the face morphing." I have seen it a few times now. People's faces will just change into something alien or demonic, even for a brief few seconds. I have even seen lizard eyes behind human eyes clicking away. It is a revelation of the being's true nature and form. It is a warning signal.

A few months into this relationship I woke up to Jack shaking me "get up! get up!" I was dizzy and all could see was blurry orange everywhere. I knew it was fire. My bedroom was on fire. I had been drugged. I grabbed the sheets off my bed and started to smother the flames, I could see Jack beside me. Most of it was out by the time the fire dept showed up. I could hear my beloved dog Dolores barking at the bottom of the stairs and people yelling outside and someone kicking in the door. I tested positive for Rohypnol at the hospital and a bottle rocket through the open bedroom window was determined to be the cause of the fire.

It was my boyfriend, I could never prove it, but I know it was him. Jack told me it was him. I had caught him doing crystal meth, and because of my experience with the monster, doing meth or other hard drugs like that was a huge deal breaker with me. I tried to get him to quit and when all attempts failed, I threatened to tell his mother if he didn't stop, and he tried to kill me.

Another time, one fight got bad. So bad that I wanted everything to end. After I took a bad beating from this boyfriend, I grabbed my 22 rifle and went to run in the back yard and kill myself. When I opened the back door, I was blinded and stopped in my tracks by the biggest brightest rainbow right in my face, it absorbed me. It wasn't Jack, it was from a female presence that I only met that one time. I didn't see her; I could just feel her love me in the bright colors of the rainbow. I just dropped to my knees and cried until I was feeling better, and the rainbow faded away. She saved my life that day, whoever she was, she was a guardian angel for sure.

Then there was the chainsaw incident. He had left, moved out after the drugging and attempted murder with the fire. I awoke to what sounded like my dirt bike starting up. I sat up to see him staring at me from across the bedroom holding a running chainsaw. I bolted out of bed, down the stairs and out the front door running and screaming down the street for someone to call 911 and he chased me with the running chainsaw for what seemed like miles and forever until the sound of it started to fade away and I realised he had gone away. Again, the police were everywhere, and I was traumatized.

Sometimes I look back at that relationship, at that time of my life and can't even believe that it was real. It truly was darkness.

I remember doing an incantation, a spell, to call on Jack. I had not seen him after the fire. I was angry and I wanted to know what I was being built for. I got nothing, no word from him at all. Later in life Jack told me I was learning the dark and about free will, choice and consequences. This chapter of my life was the darkest and deserves its own graphic horror novel. Maybe one day ill write it.

It is hard for me to hold relationships. Romantic relationships and friendships. I see everything. I see right through everyone. Even when I don't want too, I see the lies, the bullshit the inauthenticity, and the weakness no matter how much denial I try to cover it with. After the depths of literal hell, I was born to, I am not the person who will feel sorry for you and cater to your whining and weaknesses. It repulses me. I dragged myself out of hell against all the odds, and so can you. If I see you working and learning your dark for your light, I will help you with everything I have. Even after all the traumas, I hold no hate or pain (I believe) or wanting revenge anymore. I have transformed it all into power. It is all alchemy. And now being super sober square for the last few decades or so, it makes everything even more clear and that isn't easy either. I use the term "friend" very lightly. I have a lot of haters, unfortunately some of them I have called friends. Not only do I have men who stalk me, I have women too. I have a woman stalker right now. I made the mistake of bringing her on board of my Paranormal Investigation team a few years ago and after so much of her unprofessional drama, empty promises, and fraudulent claims, she was becoming a liability and I had to cut her loose. I still get threats and abusive nonsense from her. It's sad that she can not let me go, she is obsessed with me. Who was it that said, "if you have enemies, you know you are doing something right". I saw the signs; the red flags and I ignored them. Lessons to be learned, I guess. My friend Tim says she will make a good background comedy element when this book, my story is made into a movie, her lurking about threatening me and even showing up at my events, once, so far.

People, students, and clients are always trying to pressure me to "coven" with them which is funny because I don't feel pressure never mind succumb to it. I learned at a very young age because of my parents' coven experience to be extremely picky with who I shared circle with. I was born May 14, making me a double Taurus with a Scorpio Moon in the year of the Ox with a Dragon bloodline to Satanic parents that murdered my twin brother, maybe even ate him. Go ahead, try to pressure me into something, anything. Anyway, I love facilitating the moon circles, seances, classes and sabbat ceremonies and discovered quite quickly that performing these sacred events and having them open to the public was an invitation to not only practice but exchange sacred energy with some pretty damaged, sick, and weak people reminding me of what that did to my parents and how it destroyed my family. PTSD? Maybe. So, no, I don't open my personal witchcraft practices to just anyone. People are generally fear based. Back in the day, I attended moon circles facilitated by other people because I am always facilitating them myself and when doing so, I don't get to surrender into the depths of the ritual because I am "working". I remember one moon circle at the metaphysical shop that I was working at was being led by a woman who confused moon worshipping with trauma work. This one night, I was sitting across the circle from my High Priestess sister Tia who took all the Seichem initiations with me. The circle facilitator was instructing everyone to turn to the person beside them and tell them the most horrific traumatic thing that ever happened to them and then have them stand up, jump up and down and yell "I am a victim!" NO. Not on my watch. As this started to happen, Tia and I looked at each other and started to laugh hysterically. Is this really happening? Tia mouthed at me "WTF?" The circle was shut down and the facilitator was not to return. Because the toxic management at this shop handled things with avoidance, all the past warnings about this facilitator were ignored. Warnings, like after the moon circle before the one described; a patron approached the shop manager asking if there "was a support group for after the moon circles." Because she had been so traumatized. Wow. I just do my own solitary esbat worshipping after I lead for everyone else. There is so much narcissism, ego, and toxicity in the metaphysical communities, comparable to the funeral industry. Maybe it is me, I have a very low tolerance for these things.

The first thing I teach my students in spirit communications is that you can not do this work if you are scared. You must have courage. Fear is a low vibration. It is the fear when using the Ouija Board that will summon the evil, it is the fear that will backfire all your spell work and spirit conjuring. Don't summon up Uncle Bob and then run away when he shows up. I have rarely found a heart of courage to match my own. Courage is a high vibration. Low vibration can not survive in a high vibration environment.

I hold more power alone with my spirit guides than I do with others. Just like I did when I was a little girl. I've always been solitary. If I was to have an official coven, it would consist of a few true-blue people of power that I know as my students and tried and tested magical collogues. You know who you are. Over the years they have proved authentic integrity that does match my own. I am so very proud of them and to see my students embrace their psychic abilities and gifts and go on to be amazing readers, witches and mediums warms my little black heart.

MY LITTLE BLACK HEART.

Coming into my mid 20's, after the chainsaw incident and that time of my life was over, I evolved. I got into acting at that time and was hired to star in a heavy metal video for Much Music Loud where I met and fell in love on set of the video with my rockstar boyfriend and we were together for 7yrs. I went on to be in a few heavy metal videos for different bands and I met a lot of people and went to a lot of gigs.

Music has its own spirit, an energy that I can see almost like an aura, but different. Seven years of Heavy Metal band life is what ultimately made me stop drinking. It was during this time of my life that my dad died, and it was a difficult time, and I was very insecure and a total mess in those years. After my rockstar boyfriend and I split up, I made a serious effort to pursue my mortuary career and started to volunteer at a private funeral home in 2004 where I started to embalm bodies without a license. I was desperate to get into the field as it can be very difficult to land an apprenticeship. This funeral home dangled an apprenticeship in front of my face for years and I worked for them for free most of the time doing embalming, Coroner Calls (picking up bodies from all kinds of accident scenes and places) and working funerals. Again, another book needed for those early days.

Eventually they let me go because I took a job at an XXX Adult Store downtown. You can not mix sex and death I guess, "It reflects bad on the funeral home". This store was a third sex shop, a third cannabis shop and a third lingerie shop where I was assistant manager for 5 years. This is where I started to see attachments on people, the burdens they carried like sex addiction. Sex addiction sits on your back with one hand inside your head. It looks much different than the heavy shadow of drug addiction. It was one of the most fun places I have ever been employed at until it all went to hell. The porn shop, yet again, another book.

It was during this time that I moved into a haunted apartment. The very first day it started with my friend that was helping me move. He put the unplugged TV on the floor, and it turned on by itself! My friend said "oh, your apartment is haunted!" We just stared at each other. I said, "stop please!" and it turned off. But that was just the beginning. I did all the things, sage, blessed, conjured and casted. It was not long until I started to experience some of the most sever out of body and ghost experiences I have ever had. He, the ghost, would touch me. Grab my legs. Touch my face. Turn the taps on and off. I would hear him crawl over the balcony; I was on the top third floor. And when he spoke, he sounded digital.

All this was happening at the same time as the severe out of body experiences. I started to hear a dark rumbling sound, like a bowling ball as I was floating out of my body. I knew it was not good. One time, I was above my body, I could see all my bodies in layers shaking violently. I thought I was watching myself have a seizure. When I finally came out of it, I called my friend to take me to the hospital. We left there after an hour of waiting. My friend told me they would put me on the psych ward if I explained myself. The seizure I know now was myself witnessing the vibration I was stuck in between the worlds due to my resistance. Things got worse. One night, in astral, I found myself outside across the street from my apartment. It was the middle of the day. The tree in the front of the building, that now reached my balcony was much smaller and younger. I knew I was back in time. Then appeared a shirtless man in bellbottom blue jeans climbing up the balconies! He was reaching from the second-floor balcony up to mine on the third. I yelled "hey! Hey you!" He turned around to look at me right in the eyes with his big dark eyes, long dark hair, and a bearded mustache. We held the gaze for what seemed like forever and then he just fell to the ground to his death. This was the ghost in my apartment.

Through all of this, my mother was dying of cancer. I told her in our phone calls about what had been happening with the haunting and the severe out of body experiences. During one of our last phone calls, I told my mother I had had enough and was going to move, it seemed nothing I did got rid of him, meaning it wasn't my place to do so. My mother died soon after that phone call on the full moon of October(same moon as my conception) and from that very night of her death, all the paranormal and terrible out of body stuff stopped. My mom took care of the haunted apartment, the ghost and everything that went with it.

After the sex shop, I moved back home to Vancouver. I landed my teenage dream job in my 30's at my favorite shop Millenium on Granville St. downtown Vancouver. Millenium was a famous gothic, heavy metal & punk rock clothing and accessory shop. I eventually became the last manager before the owner shut it down due to extreme rent increases after 25 years of being in business. It was a very sad day when I had to hand over the keys after 5 years of being there. Oh, the stories working downtown Granville St, so many ghosts. We would keep the front door of the shop wide open, sometimes the street ghosts would come in shopping just like the living did.

I had become untouchable as far as dating during this time, my bar was so high, and I had a strict list I was sticking too and at the top of that list was #1. He must be sober. Not even one beer. Again, a PTSD response for sure. I have an amazing ability for self discipline, so I was ready to be single for the rest of my life and I was ok with that. Then one day, an old friend came to visit me at work and little did I know at the time, he brought my husband Scott with him. Scott hit everything on my check list. We were married 8 months later, October 31st, 2013. He is a very normal guy who rides a Harley, is very super sweet to our pets and was sober. He has supported all my freakshow career callings. We rented The Chapel Arts downtown Vancouver which was Vancouver's original morgue turned into an event venue. I had become friends with the facilitator for the Fetish party scene through Millennium and as a wedding gift he left all the Halloween fetish ball décor up for me to go with about 100 carved jack o lanterns that I carved with runes stones symbols and sigils, and each guest was asked to bring a carved jack as well. I had guest chairs marked and saved for all my dead friends as well as an empty bride's side for my family. My sister was my only living flesh relative there for my wedding that night. My Halloween wedding was one for the books, people are still talking about it. It was deep, scary, and authentic. It was like a demonic theater play that I wrote, choreographed, and produced myself. And of course, we were married by an 8-foot-tall Satan. I walked down the isle naked except for chains, body paint, booty shorts, horns, and security guards to my wedding march music of the band Six Feet Under's version of Venom's 'In League with Satan'. There were around 200 guests I believe. One of my best works of art for sure. There are videos of it out there. People left in shock. Perfect.

Marriage is a choice everyday, and Stevie Nicks said it best when she sang:

"Dreams unwind, loves' a state of mind."

I asked spirit recently, why so many people are alone or are unhappy and I was told that many of us come to earth without our truest loves, like we're going away to work. There is no time on the other side, so it doesn't seem like a big deal when we plan these things. When we get here to earth, we start to miss that feeling of "them" deep within our souls and start to look for who we are missing. We see glimpses of them in other people and fall in love with those pieces. Some people are fortunate and come here with their soul's mate however the rest of us have many soul mates and this creates a problem with attachments when we are supposed to let go after the lessons learned and move on. I now understand that we are supposed to love as much as we can while we are here. Again, thousands of years of programming and spiritual sabotage have messed us up.

Even in this day and age, out come the torches and pitchforks. During my last 2 Psychic Circus Fairs, my friend Jimi who lends me his land to have the events on, was receiving the same hate mail to his cell phone that I was receiving online. People threatening to burn me, to have me arrested for witchcraft, promising first class tickets to hell. Wow. I am under attack a lot for what I do. I spend a lot of time with my beasts, my beloved pets or "familiars" writing Occult classes and reading Tarot online through video messenger. My pets are my source of light, my truest loves.

I had wanted to be a vet when I was a little girl until my first pet died at 9 yrs. Old, my cat Misty was run over by a car, and I barely survived the devastation. I can deal with the human dead, process human bodies all day and bury people until the end of time and not crack a tear as I can hold courage for that type of thing, but when it comes to the innocence and pure of heart animals, I'm a mess, so I chose to be a postmortem human surgeon instead. I spend a lot of time at the gym, always have. I was about 14 when I started to work out at the gym, I realised the spirits and visions didn't bother me so much when I was working out listening to very loud music. I started teaching step aerobics and personal training right out of high school. It still is my go-to for grounding. Still not sure I really know what being truly grounded is, but I know working out helps bring me closer to Earth because I am always in 2 or 3 dimensions at once.

I have so many stories.

Men just want to kill me or own me. Not all men of course, I do have a few good male friends that are still alive. The women? Most of the women betray me. And they use me. They are threatened by my genuine call to power of the light and the dark. They're jealous. When they can't keep up, they turn on me. I am not being conceited; it is just a fact of my life. And although I always usually see it coming, as I do see the red flags, I ignore them as long as possible because I don't have very many friends, then bang, there it is. Their ugly betrayal and my cut off reaction to it. I've lost count on how many people I've told to fuck off. I know that may seem harsh, but every time I have had a moment of compassion against my better judgement of second sight, it has backfired.

Women will try to befriend me just to use me for psychic advice. You will never find my phone number on my business card however, once and a while someone gets it accidently. A person will start to dump their drama on me and then "what are you picking up on that?" or, "maybe pull a card or 2 for me" or they will book a Tarot reading with me and not pay me because they feel they have established a friendship with me and are entitled to my gifts without exchange. I have way more friends on the other side in the afterlife than I do here on Earth. We all do. Payment for psychic services is about the "exchange" of energy. I do not have the time; I choose to not have the time to listen to drama or self-inflicted sorrows. If you want spiritual advice, make a Tarot appointment with me for monetary exchange and I promise you won't hear my opinion on anything, everything I say during Tarot is from spirit. What I think and what spirit says are two totally different things.

I am always taking new clients.

Kylaedwards73@gmail.com

Tarot is so much more than the prediction of the future. Through my Tarot, I can see where my client's power may lie, I can see and hear their spirit guides, and most of the time, their light exists through their dark. Its my job to tell them that the greatest lightworkers come from the worst of the dark, that in fact you can not be a lightworker unless you are a dark worker. How are you supposed to work your light when you don't know the dark? There is so much of this toxic bullshit of "love & light" "the rule of 3" and "good vibes only". Like stated earlier, I've even had other mediums not work with me anymore because I use the word Occult and "dark worker" in my description and on my business cards. These people will run from their own shadow, never mind try to protect you from any other shadows. People are afraid of the Dark. I am not.

I also see a lot of other stuff during tarot readings that I have now asked Rebecka to protect me from. I can now know about "stuff" without seeing all the other stuff that goes along with it such as crime and humiliation. My client's privacy protection policy if you will and offering this to my clients is gold.

My opening spiel to first time clients usually goes like this:

"Do you believe in life after death or that you have spirit guides? It is your guides that will pick out your cards.

Have you ever had your traditional Tarot read before? You can think or ask whatever you want, or not say a word out loud at all, but Tarot is going to tell you what you need to hear.

Tarot is full of doom and gloom and salt and vinegar. I do not sugar coat anything and I can promise that you will not be hearing my opinion on anything. If Tarot is talking about something that makes you uncomfortable, just listen to the message and we will move on. While we do this work, we are raising our vibration, our frequencies, to meet our guides. This vibration also raises your own psychic abilities so, when tarot is describing a person, place, or thing, do not second guess what first goes through your mind. You may feel physical sensations such as chills, goosebumps, and hot and cold breezes. You may suddenly become overwhelmed with emotions. I have had the biggest toughest of guys start to cry after 2 cards down, know that this is a normal side effect from the high vibration of connecting to spirit. Please feel free to ask as many questions as you want as we go. If something is unanswered at the end we will go in deeper. Do you have any questions before we begin?"

ASTRAL

Astral travel and out of body experiences are not new to me, I've suffered with them since I can remember. I remember hanging on to the top of my bedroom door since the age of 3. I say suffer because I do not like it. My mother was also gifted with these abilities however was terrified of it, and I along with inheriting these gifts from her, I inherited her fears of it as well. She would tell me that if I left, if I went travelling, I would get lost and told me stories of being buried alive and about caskets being exhumed with scratch marks on the inside of the coffin lids from people coming back into their bodies and not being able to get out of their graves.

One night in 2018 changed my life forever.

I could feel myself start to rise out of bed, classic levitation, it happens to me all the time. And with the realization of floating up, comes the fear and panic and the trying to grasp the blankets and the bed to which I can not because I am in astral plane. I hit the ceiling and as my head turns, I saw as always, my body below. I felt my astral body start to turn with my gaze towards my body below and I realized I was starting to turn upside down. I realized that I am in front of one of the two mirrors on either side at the end of my bed. I saw in the mirror that I was shaped into an upside down cross and the image of myself begins to be replaced with a figure that is right side up. I was staring at what I first thought to be Baphomet. It was not Baphomet. It was a Devil. Black as black, a goat head with horns, deep red fire eyes, vicious tooth smile with fast wagging tongue, and hooves! Staring right at me, right through me. I was terrified. Then I heard Jack say, "My love, light the goddess within" and in that moment, I knew I was looking at my self. I was looking at the darkest version of myself. I knew I was looking at who was in the basement with me when I was 5 during that laundry episode with my mother. I knew I was looking at my Dark. This beast in the mirror was me. Knowing that she is inside of me, I have never been afraid of anything ever again.

I never liked astral travelling; I always hated it. I am trying so very hard now to embrace the gift. I believe it is the exit and re-entering of my body that I have a problem with. I don't always realize or remember the leaving my body part. Once I am out and about, it is fine. It used to leave me disoriented for days after, but I have been getting better with the hangover through time. I've had hundreds of experiences. Have you ever seen the movie Doctor Sleep? It is the sequel to The Shining. In Doctor Sleep, The gypsy witch, Rose, astral travels into outer space on the Earth's edge. I can do that. I do it all the time. I had tears running down my face the first time I saw it depicted in the movie. I had never seen it outside of myself until that moment. Sometimes I hang out in a spot between the Earth and the Moon, and I just listen to the universe. I hear the vibrations, I hear the planets, and I hear other life. It is amazing but terrifying. When I am at this spot in space, I feel I am closer to home. My true home is beyond the 3rd dimension of Earth. I feel I am from the Horse Head Nebula, through Orion's Belt.

In astral travel, the star constellations swirl and create patterns. I see star gates. One high windy warm summer cloudless night, a friend and I went to star gaze on the cliffs on the edge of the forest over a lake. I swear we could see every single star. As we were sitting out on the cliff under the stars, I saw them. I saw 2 stargates open in the starry night sky. Big electric blue circles opened right above me. I was seeing them for the first time here on Earth and I wasn't astral travelling.

Last year I had a terrifying vision in one of my outer space hang outs. I was comfortably floating in between the 3D Earth and the new 5D Earth and that's when I saw the 4D Earth. It was our beautiful 3D Earth and coming up over it was a black cloud of tar like goo, like the thing in the VGH morgue, swallowing it up. It was so sad and so full of despair. I saw souls being stuck beneath me in like a spider web, they were trying to get into the new 5th dimension Earth and couldn't, they were trapped in the in between.

I know I am here to try to prevent this from happening by spreading awareness. I came out of trance and started looking up information on a 5th dimension Earth or other people describing similar visions and that's where I found Dolores Cannon. I think I have now read everything she published. I think about 80% of what I have read I already knew; I had already seen these things and places myself. There was a lot of conformation for me there. The 20% that didn't really sit with me was based on other people's perception of things, and perception is a powerful thing.

I love to honor the Sabbats and Esbats through Pagan ritual, I love connecting with the ancient Pagan ways of life. The past Spring, I had moved across the ocean from Steveston straight to Vancouver Island and had an amazing summer with a new friend Tim who I had met while working a psychic fair the year before. Tim is an amazing remote viewer and psychic. He and I went to the ocean side cliffs at Neck Point Park in Nanaimo, BC, so I could lead and film the Mabon Sabbat for my Facebook and Tik Tok followers during the Fall Equinox ritual I was performing on the last day of the summer. Although these Sabbats are for having gratitude and not for asking favors, I did state out loud that my only regret of the summer was not seeing the Orcas. My whole life spent on the west coast, and I had never seen them. It seemed I had always just missed them whenever I went to the beach all that summer. As I finished the ritual, I looked up at the sunset on the Ocean and saw water spray, I could not believe it, there they were. A family of 4 Orca's. A huge father, a mother and 2 little baby Orcas up so close and personal. I was surged with emotion as I knew it was a gift for me from the universe. It was magic. I earned some credibility with my new friend Tim that day.

Pictures of the Orcas are from the internet however the picture of me was during the Mabon Fall Equinox Ritual

THE BEASTS OWN MY HEART

The first time I "gate jumped" I was about 9 years old after my cat Misty, my first pet had been killed by a car. I focused so hard on seeing him again, I left my body and crossed the starlight bridge into a lush landscape and there he was. I held him and I could hear him say "We come as Earth Angels, and Angels we will always be. I will never leave you" and I know that our pets never leave us, even after death.

My Dolores Charlotte, my true love, my dog daughter.

February 04,1994 - October 18,2009.

When my then roommate, Xave's dog, accidently got pregnant because Ricky had left a door open, I was excited. I was going to get a puppy. I rubbed mama dog's tummy every day saying, "I want a little white one with brown ears". Xave knew that I practiced magic however he often made fun of me for this. Then when mama dog had her puppies, and well would you look at that, all white puppy twins both with brown ears! Later that day, one of the twins passed away. Just like me. I was left with my Dolores. Xave never questioned me after that. Dolores was my soulmate. She lived a lot of life with me, sometimes she was the only one that kept me alive, she was my reason. When she passed away in my arms from kidney disease at 15, in October of 2008 I felt her soul melt into mine. I absorbed her.

Dolores Charlotte

Creeper Jones, my cat was born on October 31st, 2009.

He is pure black, his front paws measure 2 inches across, and his head is 3 times the size of any other cat I have ever seen. At his peak at 10 years old he weighed in at 27 lbs. Everyone that has met him, "wow, that's a big cat". You would think such a creature born on Halloween would be tough and own the night however he is the biggest suck and afraid of his own shadow. Mama's boy. He is 15 years old and very healthy as I write this. Between Creeper Jones and Dolores, they have been my longest and truest loves.

Creeper Jones

Kordeilia Babeechka Figini, my beloved cat passed away at 14 from cancer in 2017. Her loss was devastating. My husband brought home a little black kitten surprise a few days later. I wasn't ready for a "replacement" cat. We named her Wednesday Tuesday. It didn't take me that long to fall in love again. I took a picture of Wednesday on the bed and later looked at the picture to see a huge orb beside her, right where Kordeilia used to sleep. It was for sure Kordeilia, letting me know she was around and approved of little Wednesday Tuesday.

Wednesday & Dorothy

Tarot Etc. I Am Witch.

Kordeilia's Orbs

THE RABBITS.

MY MOTHER LOVED RABBITS. SHE ALWAYS said they were a favorite of the Fae, and if rabbits were around, so were faeries. She taught us to always be kind and to love the buns, hence why she was horrified during the baby bunny necromancy attempt when I was a little girl. I have a picture of my mother with her pet rabbit when she was young and still living in England framed in the cabinet. One day, Scott had forgotten his keys and had come through to the back of the house to get them and said, "there's a rabbit out here". I ran outside and just scooped the poor little rabbit up. The vet said she was about a year old. Someone just let her go, abandoned her, and she obviously knew where to go after that. My house.

Phoxie Bunn was amazing little Harlequin bunny. She was litter trained on the first day and I never caged her or restricted her, she lived in the house like one of the cats and we loved her very much. The first week she lived with us, I started to have visions of another little black rabbit, Phoxie's baby brother. This led to arguments about all the animals we already had living in our condo. When Phoxie was about 4, we were driving home from grocery shopping and as always, there were rabbits everywhere in that part of town. I told Scott to pull over the truck to see them and said, "I am going to get Phoxie's little brother" to which he replied sarcastically "if you can catch one you can keep it". Like I would need his permission! I sat down on the grass and said out loud "If any of you want to come home with me, now is the time" and this little, tiny black rabbit ran straight for me from under a bush! I thought to myself that he would take off when I went to pick him up, but he didn't. He looked at me and blinked twice and all I heard in that moment was "Mama." I held him close and looked over at Scott in the truck and all he said was "get in the truck" and that's how I got my little Ouija B.

Kyla A. N. Edwards

If you want to help abandoned bunnies, please contact

info@rabbitats.org

Phoxie Bunn

Tarot Etc. I Am Witch.

Ouija B.

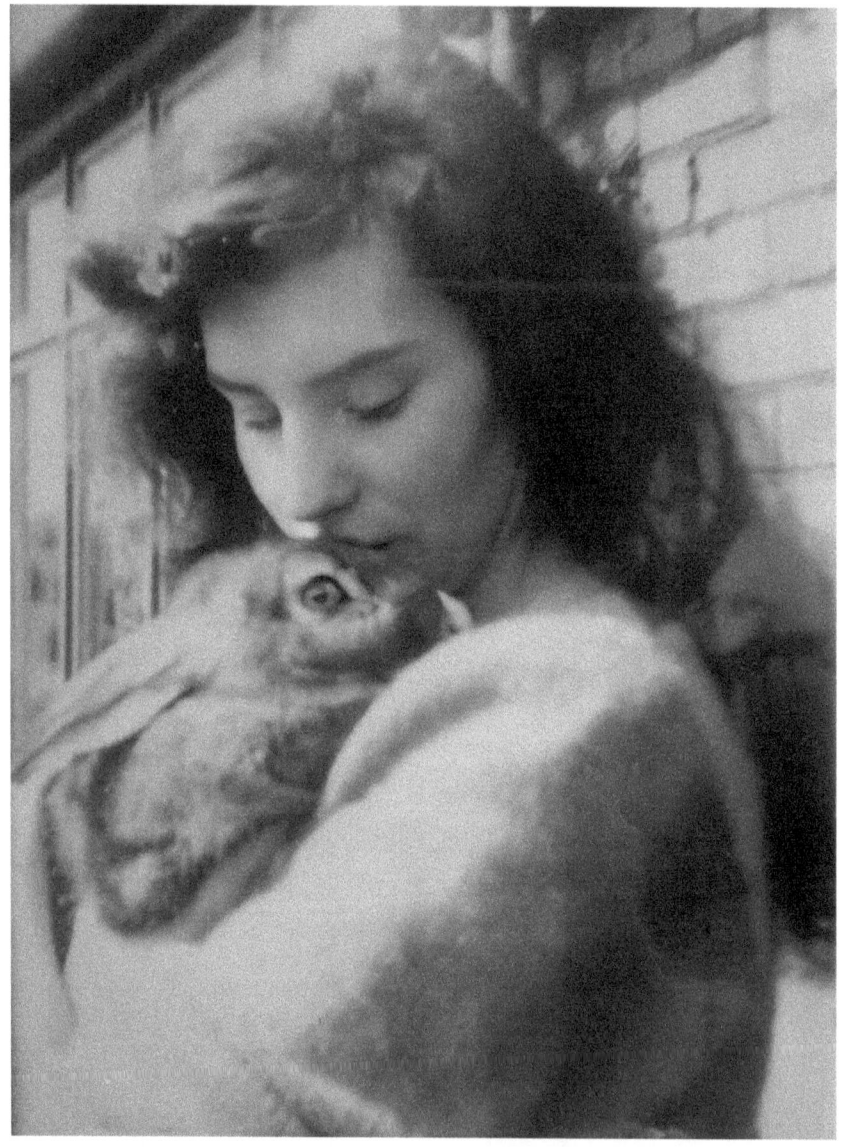

Mother & her rabbit in England

Phoxie passed away suddenly 2 years later leaving Ouija B. to be raised further by his cat siblings, Creeper Jones and Wednesday Tuesday. It is my mother's spirit sending me the rabbits. And my dad? My dad sent me a crow.

MASTER KASPER

MASTER KASPER HAD THE WORST START to his precious life. He showed me in a vision that he fell from the nest during one of the worst rainstorms we had ever had in our part of the world and nature, being brutal as it is, Kasper's parents thought they would do him a favor and try to kill him. They pecked out his left eye in an attempt to end his life. They failed. This little baby crow in terrible shape found his way to me. I called all the wildlife rehab centers and all four of them in my district just wanted to euthanize him, they wouldn't even accept sponsorship for his recovery. So, he didn't go anywhere. My amazing vet, one of my favorite people on this planet, and my dear Crow Witch from up north, helped me nurse Kasper back to health. I taught him to fly, healed his damaged wing and missing eye and he became a strong healthy boy, and I'm his mother now. He visits me often.

Master Kasper

Currently, all my beasts match. All 4 of them are pitch black. I only worry when they arrange themselves in shapes such as squares, circles, and triangles.

If you love crows and ravens, please, if possible, donate to my Northern Crow Witch. She has dedicated her life to building her own crow and raven rescue and rehab.

Good Caws Crow Rescue Society

goodcaws@outlook.com

EGYPT

I HAVE STUDIED SEICHEM. SEICHEM IS A form of universal energy that was used for healing purposes in Ancient Egypt. This energy heals on the physical, emotional, mental, and spiritual levels with a focus on the heart center. It is like Reiki but operates on a higher vibration and heals on a deeper level as Reiki is just one element, the earth element, where as Seichem uses all four elements. Air, Earth, Fire and Water.

I am a third degree Seichem priestess. I completed initiation with the Violet Flame given in the first degree. I have completed and received the initiation of YOD in my second degree. This develops psychic abilities and connects the Seichem healer with the Ancient Egyptian light workers.

These initiations brought me to my achievement with the highest honors as High Priestess of the Melchizedek (pre – Christian), following in alignment with our higher beings who work to fulfil the divine plan of earth. I am all of these things and more without the formal initiations of someone else's organized process however it was fun and I'm a lover of formal ritual anything. I completed the Seichem High Priestess initiations with a good friend Tia who is now my High Priestess sister, and we now share this connection and now seem to parallel with life events.

I have been a woman in all my past lives here on earth, and I have been here a very long time. I am very much feminine energy. I can recall two past lives in Ancient Egypt. These lives are obviously where I acquired my embalming skills, alchemic abilities and developed my passion for the dead and my love for Anubis.

In one Ancient Egyptian life, I can recall being a little girl at the age of six. I am on the edge of the river Nile making mud dollies while my mother is doing the laundry. I remember my mother smiling at me under the warm sun as I carved dresses into the mud of the dolls with a stick. I knew I was going to grow up and make dresses for the Queen of Egypt. I can see my long dark soft curls highlighted with gold in the sun hanging past my arms as I drew dresses on the mud dolls.

In the other Egyptian life that I remember, I was a grown woman. I was hosting the funeral of my sister's second husband at my house. I was sitting in a chair in a room by myself off to the side of where all the guests were. The doors were all open, and I could see the water of the Nile in the distance and feel the warm breeze blowing through my open home. It was mid day. I could hear the people talking, see the long tables full of food and drinks with the white sheer material blowing in the breeze separating the rooms. It was a very large place. The floors were white marble and looking down I could see my toenails were polished and shiny and I was wearing very fine gold chain bracelets and anklets. I feel I am about the age of 42 and of high social standing. I can see my long black hair flowing over the left side of my body past my breasts. Things were calm and peaceful however I felt bad for my sister.

Now, I am trained and facilitate other people's past life regression sessions. It is amazing to witness and experience so many lives and stories. I can use remote viewing to see into their lives as they are recalling them. It is amazing.

My students

There is a "Baby Witch" movement, people of all ages finding their way to magic and their psychic abilities. Some of it I love with all my heart, and some of it I do not, for instance I don't like the limiting casual terminology and all the limiting rules. Yes, I am a Witch since birth, however, please do not ever reference me or my life's work as "witchy". The term seems immature to me.

"Witchy" suggests "witch - like".

I am not "witch-like."

I am Witch. My mother was Witch. My father was Witch. Hardcore.

"Witchy " denotes a lack of formal integrity that I require and deserve.

And I pass this on to my students. Yes, there are some basic guidelines for energy manipulation however, I throw rules, attachments and limiting beliefs right out the window. Each student I mentor is unique, and each one needs to be mentored differently. Witchcraft comes from the heart of the witch and no two hearts are the same. I teach the manipulation of energy to your favor, what the student does with it is up to them.

So many have sat before me at the tarot table, either live or on the screen thinking they are crazy, they are in trouble and in a terrible desperate state and in need of help. I see what I can only describe as sparkles on people, within their aura when they too have extreme psychic abilities. So many times, I deliver the good news "you are not crazy, you are psychic". I then sometimes I have the great honor of training and guiding them to becoming amazing psychic mediums and talented witches. It is extremely satisfying. It is part of my mission here on Earth. There is a casting call across the universe to bring souls to Earth currently for the sole purpose of raising the Earth's vibration, I do my part one Tarot reading at a time, one student at a time. The Earth, as we do, has a spirit. She, the Earth, has had enough of the low vibration of what has been happening here for over a thousand years, and it is killing her. Low vibration can not survive in high vibration environment and vice versa. The Earth wants to leave her body and reawaken into the 5th dimension, a new state of high vibration consciousness. The separation between these dimensions, the 3rd, and the 5th, is happening right now. We are at spiritual war.

About 10 years ago, I noticed Tarot was giving The Empress and Emperor cards to very young clients. Jack explained that these were evolved souls, star seeds, which have come here with the highest of soul vibrations to help with the spiritual war. Now, these star seeds are suffering. They are so highly evolved that they don't fit in, they have trouble forming relationships and they don't know how to process their human emotions. Jack explained "it isn't because they are new souls, it is because they are new to Earth" Earth is the hardest dimension in the entire universe. It is the only place we suffer from pain, from flesh bodies and experience hate and illness. Earth is hard. Not all souls were allowed to come here at this time. So, consider yourself special and know you have a part to play in saving the spirit of the Earth if you are here. This war is my mission; it is why I am here. It is why I survived through so much darkness since the moment I arrived.

Like I have already stated, I am not a satanist, however being raised as one, I still follow some of the 11 Satanic rules of the Earth, not on purpose, they just feel right and are a part of my personality.

THE ELEVEN SATANIC RULES OF THE EARTH

1. **Do not give opinions or advice unless you are asked.** (Yes)
2. **Do not tell your troubles to others unless you are sure they want to hear them.** (Yes)
3. **When in another's lair, show him respect or else do not go there.** (Yes)
4. **If a guest in your lair annoys you, treat him cruelly and without mercy.** (Yes, do not disrespect me in my castle)
5. **Do not make sexual advances unless you are given the mating signal.** (Yes)
6. **Do not take that which does not belong to you unless it is a burden to the other person, and he cries out to be relieved.** (Yes)
7. **Acknowledge the power of magic if you have employed it successfully to obtain your desires. If you deny the power of magic after having called upon it with success, you will lose all you have obtained.** (Yes, take no credit, take no blame. People praise me about my psychic talents, and I am quick to enlighten them that it is in fact not me, it is THEM)
8. **Do not complain about anything to which you need not subject yourself.** (Yes)
9. **Do not harm little children.** (Yes of course, however I have a problem with this being here because of my brother. Do new babies not count as "little children"? What's the loophole?)
10. 10. **Do not kill non-human animals unless you are attacked or for your food.** (I am Vegan, well 98% and have always used not tested on animal products. I am also as sober square as you can get for my own personal empowerment)
11. **When walking in open territory, bother no one. If someone bothers you, ask him to stop. If he does not stop, destroy him.** (Yes. Get them before they get you)

— by Anton Szandor LaVey ©1967

I have been reading traditional tarot now going on to 42 years.

I was fortunate to have parents, no matter what mistakes they made, who recognized my psychic abilities and encouraged and supported them. It doesn't matter what my parents did, I wouldn't trade them for anything being who I am today. I explain to my clients when they get The Judgement card (which should be renamed as The Spiritual awakening card), or The Devil and especially when they get The Devil combined with Temperance, it is about spiritual evolution. The Devil is a lightworker card because he is a dark worker and again, you need to be both if you are to be a powerful witch or powerful anything else. With Judgement, its about being accountable. It is about suffering through our stuff properly because we all know there are ways to not suffer constructively.

In the end, no one judges us on the other side, we judge ourselves, and I use that a lot when explaining to earthbound spirits that its safe for them to cross over. When we can look back through our life and see where we have put ourselves in the path of the dark and through hell by the choices we have made, when we are accountable, we get to rise. When we can look back even further to all the terrible things that happened to us when we were little kids and bring that darkness and pain into balance with the light, we get to rise in our power. And rising isn't easy as we leave a lot behind. It is all free will, choice, and consequences. It is a breakthrough transformation of spiritual evolution requiring us to leave parts of ourselves and other people we love behind. Rebecka showed me that as we rise, to the left of us is a tar pit, a big circle of sludge and people we love are in there walking around and around in circles. They will never be accountable for anything. Constantly playing the blame game, falling to drugs and alcohol, and refusing to do anything to help themselves. These are people we love however these are people that can not rise with you, and they will always try to keep you in the pit with them and every time you fall to meet them, you make yourself sick and heavy to the point where you will stop rising being loaded with their sickness and if you don't rise to your calling, you will lose your opportunity and you have failed. A lot of the suffering we experience, anxiety and depression belong to other people. It is a brutal side effect of being an authentic empath. It's a gift, it is a curse if you don't master that ability.

Yes, I tell it how it is, I don't sugar coat anything. The same toxic metaphysical manager that was watching readings through the security camera once told me to remove all the "bad & scary" cards from my deck, we all know how that went over. The good thing is even when Tarot is telling you hard things, it always gives you an exit plan, a silver lining and I always finish with that.

2023 was the year of The Tower for me and so many others. It was shown to me like we were all in a bag that had been shaken up and then we were tossed like dice and thrown hard to the ground. I believe it was some kind of energetic collision to get the ball rolling for the shift into the 5th dimension.

For the rest of that year, I was receiving messages and scheduling Tarot appointments and spirit council meetings for my students and seasoned witches and mediums alike asking me "what the fuck is going on?" In total there was five talking about suicide and two had checked themselves into the psyche hospital for mental health. This energetic collision had everyone second guessing themselves. But not me. Jack told me exactly what it was.

That April when my Tower started to burn, my soul absorbed the power and the fury like never before and here it comes as always, the creative downloads from spirit. Spirits started to tell me to paint again after 10 years of not picking up a paint brush. "Paint the Tower" repeatedly burned through my mind. I was consumed so then I did. I poured all the devastation of my own Tower incident into the painting. It was the beginning of my Tarot painting empowerment series. Spirits will repeatedly deal me the same card in real time and in my mind to the point of obsession until I paint it with the magic and power of that card. I will start to paint it and as soon as I post the beginning of the painting on social media, its owner will contact me to purchase it before I am even done. It is that client who I am painting it for that needs the power of that tarot card.

I really need to author another book for my deep lifelong relationship with Tarot. The Tower. Yes, it is the scariest looking card in the deck however, it truly is a blessing in disguise. When we are building on falsehood, unsafe ground, eventually the ground will break collapsing everything with it. Before this happens, the universe will send signs so we can correct this in time for ourselves, it will send us the red flags and most of the time, we will ignore them and that's when the universe will send down the lightning bolt and do it for you which is usually a devastating and extremely traumatic event. So, when the Tower shows up in a reading, I tell my client that they have a few choices now that they know it is on the way.

1. You can ignore it and let it happen
2. You can try to prepare for it and get out of the way or
3. Grab the gas can and light it up yourself. Burn baby burn.

The good news is that after the fire and the smoke has cleared, you will have new ground to rebuild. It is always a blessing in disguise.

And the Death card? Good news. That is you, you are that Reaper riding that Death horse. Start slaying.

I am an occultist, a daughter of an occultist, an occult teacher, a master of the Tarot. I am a paranormal Investigator and a professional death care provider practicing psychic mediumship. I facilitate witchcraft circles and moon ceremonies. I live in and manipulate the energies around me. It's all alchemy.

The Tower

From entertaining my parents' friends, being the creepy weird girl in High School since elementary school when made to stand in the hallway during the Lord's prayer, to reading at the night clubs in my bar star days...to reading for a world famous entertainment company that sent me to major corporate events and high end estate parties which I do now for myself with my business Tarot Etc. (including my childhood school district's corporate events Who is standing in the hallway now Mrs. B?!) to countless metaphysical shops, psychic fairs including ones I produce myself as Tarot Etc. Psychic Circus fairs, to home parties, now to ZOOM and Facebook Video Messenger, to live lectures and presentation on the Occult and the paranormal, teaching witchcraft and reading Tarot around the World. *I have clients across the world. I have gone global!*

I can't wait to see what my "Crone" years hold for my beloved Tarot & I.

Tarot. It is my calling, and it will keep calling.

I have dedicated my life to the mystic arts and writing my own classes such as Tarot, Scrying, Psychic Development, Moonology, Paranormal and Occult lectures and presentations, Past Life Regression, Candle Magic, Spell Casting, Spirit Communications and Ouija Board and Seance lessons etc. etc. etc. I have taken so much flack for the name of my company, Tarot Etc. It has had its name for over 20 years now and haters have it made it clear that they don't like it. People have often approached me to changing my image, to softening it up for business success. It will never happen. I am who I am.

In Mortuary school, we had to write a big deal presentation for a hefty percentage of our final grade. It had to be funeral industry related of course. I decided to do mine on the afterlife and how it helps or hinders the grieving process. I included my own paranormal investigation evidence from my trips to New Orleans and Salem Massachusetts etc. and it was approved by the board. I was approached by two different classmates and my funeral home manager not to do it. They warned me that it would damage my reputation, and no one would hire me, that it would be "frowned" upon by the industry. I did it anyway and received 88% on it.

A decade later, I realised I had the foundation of my "Enchanted Evening of the Paranormal" lecture and presentation showcasing all my favorite haunts and experiences. This led me to writing my lecture on the Occult to which became the bones of this book. My parents and Jack are proud of me.

I look back and now understand my path, I understand why things unfolded as they did. I needed it all and everything to be me, to be who I am now and stand in my authentic power and purpose. I have no regrets and question nothing.

I AM WITCH.

Printed in the USA
CPSIA information can be obtained
at www.ICGtesting.com
LVHW061114010424
775863LV00001B/2